Cross-Step Waltz

A Dancer's Guide

Richard Powers
Nick & Melissa Enge

Redowa Press

Copyright © 2019
by Richard Powers, Nick Enge, and Melissa Enge

ISBN-13: 978-0-9827995-7-4

First Edition

Cover Illustration by
Manuel Avendano

www.crossstepwaltz.com

Redowa Press
Stanford, CA

Contents

Welcome to the World of Cross-Step Waltz! — 1

The Story Behind Cross-Step Waltz — 3

How to Get the Most from this Book — 7

The Basics — 13

No Contest — 21

Inside and Outside Turns — 23

How to Change Your Story — 31

Lead Goes Variations — 33

Connection — 39

Empathy — 41

Grapevine Variations — 43

Avoiding Boredom — 55

Variations Inspired by Tango — 57

Mistakes — 65

Don't Mind the Mess-Ups — 67

Musicality in Cross-Step Waltz — 69

Conversations — 77

The French Valse Boston — 79

Dancing Through Differences — 85

Zig-Zag Variations — 87

How Following Works (and How Leading Can) — 91

Pivot Variations	101
Active Following	111
Cradle Position Variations	119
Empathetic Leading	129
Shadow Position Variations	135
Putting the Social in Social Dance	149
Ways to Conclude a Waltz with Flair	151
The Beauty in the Good Enough	157
The Cross-Step Waltz Mixer and Variations	159
Advantages of Cross-Step Waltz	163
Creativity in Cross-Step Waltz	165
Role Reversal in Cross-Step Waltz	171
Analogies for Leading and Following	179
Creative Interpretations	183
Dancing Down the Ski Slope	191
Cross-Step Waltz in Other Timings	193
Letting It Happen	197
Transitions to Other Dances	199
Work and Play	205
Bluesy Waltz / Waltz Fusion	207
Discography of Cross-Step Waltz Music	221
About the Authors	223
Acknowledgments	226

Welcome to the World of Cross-Step Waltz!

Cross-Step Waltz is more than a dance step. Cross-Step Waltz embodies a partnering dynamic, a mindset, and a philosophy.

The essential aspects of Cross-Step Waltz, for both the Lead and Follow, are:

> connection,
>
> > creativity,
> >
> > > flexibility,
> > >
> > > > adaptability,
> > > >
> > > > > individuality,
> > > > >
> > > > > > musicality,
> > > > > >
> > > > > > > and responsive riffing,
> > > > > > >
> > > > > > > > with kindness.

All of these are discussed in detail in this book. The first and last aspects are especially important, because Cross-Step Waltz is a noncompetitive social dance, and the key elements of any truly social dance are connection and kindness, through attentive partnering.

> "Kindness is more important than wisdom,
> and the recognition of this is the beginning of wisdom."
>
> — Theodore Isaac Rubin

Cross-Step Waltz is one of the newest social dance forms, spreading quickly because it's easy to learn yet endlessly innovative, satisfying for both beginners and experienced dancers.

In addition to being danced across the United States, Cross-Step Waltz is popular around the world. There is now an official Russian Cross-Step Waltz Federation, with several Cross-Step Waltz festivals in Russia each year. It is also danced as part of the public square dancing movement in China and can still be seen in its historical birthplace, France.

> "Fun is fundamental.
> There is no way around it.
> You absolutely must have fun.
> Without fun, there is no enthusiasm.
> Without enthusiasm, there is no energy.
> Without energy, there are only shades of gray."
>
> — Douglas Hall

Chapter 1

The Story Behind Cross-Step Waltz

Cross-Step Waltz has a curious history. When I (Richard) began teaching at Stanford University in 1992, most of my classes were in contemporary social dance, but I occasionally taught weekend workshops in historical dances like the Mazurka Waltz, Bohemian National Polka, and the Jazz Age dances of 1920s Paris. Then, once a month, I ran a student dance party called Jammix (still going strong to this day).

I noticed an unusual dance step at Jammix in 1995. I was playing "You Make Me Feel So Young" a foxtrot by Frank Sinatra, and two of my students, James Mendoza and George Yang, were traveling around the room with their partners while rotating. Distinctively, their feet were crossing through the frame on every third step. I could immediately see how creative this dance could be.

I began experimenting with this new dance. Since every third step crossed over, I changed the rhythm from 4/4 to 3/4—simply dancing that step to slow waltz music—and it worked even better. I also found that it was more musical when the Lead begins with the right foot (Follow's left), because the step with the greatest emphasis then falls on the musical downbeat. I loved the effortless flow of this new waltz, the ease of spontaneous creativity, the more equal Lead/Follow dynamic, and its gentle tempo. I decided to call it "Cross-Step Waltz."

"You Make Me Feel So Young" was a bit too fast at 124 bpm, but International Standard Waltz, at 84 to 90 bpm, was far too slow. I found that waltz music at 112-118 bpm was ideal, because that's a natural walking tempo, and I started collecting waltz music in that tempo range.

Working with my teaching partner Angela Amarillas, I developed a set of Cross-Step Waltz variations, and began teaching Cross-Step Waltz in 1996. But that isn't the end of the story.

Field Research

The following year, while I was teaching at a vintage dance week in Prague, I was surprised to see a French couple, Jean-François Lafitte and Andrée Gamelin, dancing Cross-Step Waltz exactly as I had been doing it, including beginning with the Lead's right foot. I asked them where they learned it, and they said they had been dancing this "Valse Boston" for a long time. A second couple, Sylvie and Jean-Pierre Orgeret from Lyon, were also dancing this cross-step style of Valse Boston.

Another French dancer, Josette Courtade, reported that she first danced this cross-step Valse Boston in the 1940s, and I danced it with her in Paris several times between 1998 and 2012, when she was in her 80s. Once I knew that this dance predated James Mendoza and George Yang by generations, I could search through my dance manuals and periodicals for clues.

Historical Cross-Step Waltz

Cross-steps in general became popular on the dance floor in the early 20th century. In 1914, the "Cross Walk Boston" waltz created by Frank H. Norman foreshadowed Cross-Step Waltz, but most of the early cross-step variations were in 4/4 time, in the One Step, Tango, and Foxtrot, for example. In particular, the March 1920 issue of the *Dancing Times* of London reported that in the Foxtrot, "The crossing of the feet is popular and effective."

A three-step version of the Foxtrot was popular immediately after World War I and through the 1920s. It was a repeating pattern of three steps danced in quick-quick-slow timing, called The Jazz in London. Variations included steps like the Straight Jazz and the Jazz-Roll.

In 1919, "Monsieur Pierre" described a Jazz Valse, writing: "A new form of valsing, derived from the Jazz, is rapidly gaining popularity. It is danced especially to slow and accentuated music. The steps are the same as the Straight Jazz and Jazz-Roll, with a step to every beat." This means dancing the three Foxtrot steps evenly in slow waltz time. English dance master Geoffrey D'Egville suggested the same thing in 1919. Dancing the Jazz Valse using crossed Foxtrot steps results in Cross-Step Waltz in the manner that has been revived today.

A second evolution of Cross-Step Waltz happened in Paris. Americans brought their dances—One Steps, Foxtrots, and Blues—to Paris during the 1920s, and several French dance manuals described each American dance and variation in detail. Through these dance manuals, we can see a Blues step that the French called Fox-Blues evolve through that decade, year-by-year. (For descriptions of these evolving steps, see "The French Valse Boston" on p. 81.) The cross-step appeared in the mid-20s, in the Pas Titubé ("staggering step"), and evolved into a cross-step Fox-Blues by the end of the decade. That same step could easily be danced as a waltz, when slow waltz music became popular around 1930.

We can't know for sure whether the version danced by Josette, Jean-François, and other French dancers evolved from the 1920s Fox-Blues, or if it came from the 1919 Jazz Valse. Either way, we know that it was being danced in France around that time.

In a nutshell, the cross-step Valse Boston was a vernacular dance, passed on from dancer to dancer, and occasionally mentioned in magazine articles, but it was never officially adopted by professional dance masters or authors of dance manuals. Fortunately, some French dancers continued to dance this cross-step Valse Boston to this day.

Years later, I asked James Mendoza where he first learned that dance. He replied, "I learned it from you. Remember that workshop that you taught on the Jazz Age dances of 1920s Paris? I especially liked the cross-step Fox-Blues." He had only learned the basic step in that workshop, then found it easy to innovate variations, as did I. And I found it natural to dance it as a waltz. It came together quite effortlessly, as if it were meant to be.

That 1920s Fox-Blues step apparently evolved into Cross-Step Waltz twice—once around 1930, and again in 1995.

Cross-Step Waltz Today

Since I started teaching Cross-Step Waltz in 1996, my graduating Stanford students have carried it to many different states and countries, and I've been teaching it nationally and internationally for decades. Mirroring the success of other revived vintage dances, Cross-Step Waltz is even more popular today than it was when it first appeared 100 years ago.

Since its revival, dancers around the world have invented over 500 different variations of Cross-Step Waltz. In this book, you'll find detailed explanations and videos of more than 250 of those variations, described and illustrated with the help of two of my former students—now my colleagues teaching at the University of Texas—Nick and Melissa Enge.

We hope you enjoy dancing Cross-Step Waltz as much as we do!

"Dance is for everybody.
I believe that dance came from the people
and that it should always be delivered back to the people."

— Alvin Ailey

Chapter 2

How to Get the Most from this Book

As the title suggests, this book is a dancer's guide to all things Cross-Step Waltz, including the dance, the music, and the mindset. Here are some tips for getting the most from this book.

Dance Descriptions

The majority of the pages in this book are devoted to detailed descriptions of over 250 variations of Cross-Step Waltz. If you haven't heard that term before, a "variation" is one particular sequence of movements in a dance: the terms "figure," and more colloquially, "move" (short for "dance move") are synonyms.

By reading these descriptions, you will learn all of the most satisfying, "top shelf" Cross-Step Waltz variations that have been discovered over the past two-and-a-half decades. There are hundreds more, but these are the ones that have stood the test of time and are commonly seen on the dance floor today.

Here's a sample description from Chapter 19:

Swingout [SWO]

(1-2-3) The Lead sends the Follow out to swingout position on (1), gently sweeping her past him with his right arm, immediately releasing that arm, keeping her right hand in his left. The Follow dances the first half of a non-turning basic.

(4-5-6) The Lead sweeps the Follow back into closed position by drawing his left hand back toward him. The Follow dances the second half of a non-turning basic into his arms.

Abbreviations and Conventions

While we've tried to write our descriptions as clearly as possible, avoiding unnecessary jargon, there are several key abbreviations and conventions we use throughout the book.

The numbers in parentheses refer to the counts of the music: **(1-2-3)** means "on counts 1, 2, and 3." Sometimes a longer series of counts will be abbreviated like **(1-6)**, which means "on counts 1 through 6."

For the sake of efficiency, not all steps are explicitly described. Unless otherwise specified, assume you're always taking one step per beat, keeping your feet under your body as you move through the figure. In addition, unless otherwise specified, assume you're continuously traveling along LOD.

LOD means Line of Dance, also known as Line of Direction. In this and other traveling dances, LOD is the traditional CCW path of travel around the dance floor, as in a racetrack. **Along LOD** means you're moving or facing CCW around the room, and **against LOD** means you're moving or facing CW around the room.

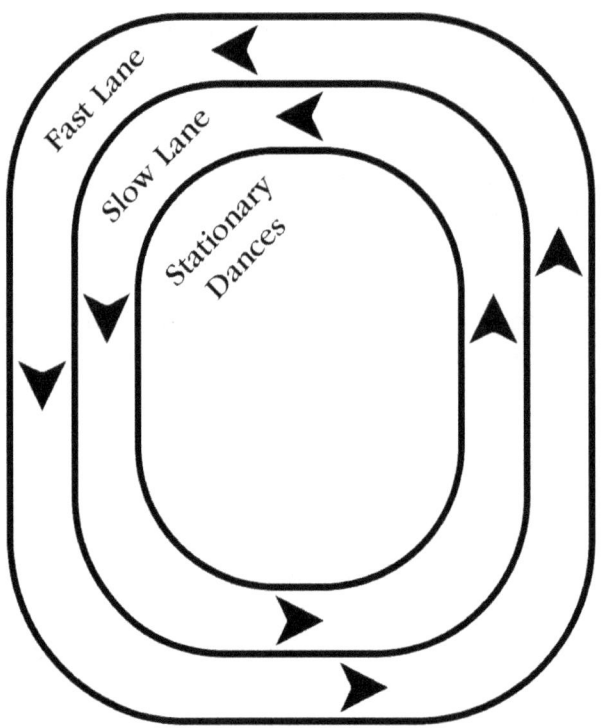

Line of Dance (LOD)

On that note, **CW** means clockwise and **CCW** means counterclockwise. Note that the clock in question is a clock on the floor, not on the ceiling.

When two dancers are traveling along LOD, the **inside lane** is the path of travel on the left side, closer to the center of the room. The **outside lane** is the path of travel on the right side, closer to the outside wall. The **track** is the exact path along LOD. Therefore, **across the tracks** means crossing from the inside lane to the outside lane, or vice versa.

L means "left foot" and **R** means "right foot." Left and right will be spelled out when referring to the left and right side, or the left and right hand.

If you're flipping through the book and encounter another word or phrase you don't know the meaning of, chances are it's been defined earlier in the book. Check in the introduction to that chapter or previous chapters, or in the descriptions of other variations that appeared shortly before that one.

When a term is capitalized, such as Turning Basic, it refers to a particular variation described elsewhere in the book. Therefore, while "Lead's underarm turn" could refer to any underarm turn for the Lead, "Lead's Underarm Turn" is a specific variation described on p. 36.

When connected hands are described as "left-to-right" or "right-to-left," the first hand is the Lead's and the second hand is the Follow's, i.e., "left-to-right" mean's Lead's left, Follow's right.

Finally, the **Lead** is the dancer who is leading at the moment, and the **Follow** is the dancer who is following. In the past, most men chose to lead and most women chose to Follow, but in Cross-Step Waltz, there is no assumption that men Lead and women Follow. Anyone can dance either role and anyone can dance with anyone.

Some people use the terms "Leader" and "Follower," but we prefer "Lead" and "Follow" for several reasons. First, they're more efficient to say when you remove the unnecessary "-er" at the end. But more importantly, the terms "Leader" and "Follower" have both dictionary definitions and social connotations that inaccurately describe the egalitarian nature of the modern Lead-Follow dynamic. We also prefer to capitalize the names of the roles, Lead and Follow, to clearly differentiate the roles from their corresponding verbs, lead and follow.

On the Use of "He" and "She"

While anyone can dance in either role, the structure of the English language requires us to use pronouns to teach efficiently. For example, without pronouns, the first sentence of the Swingout description above becomes: "The Lead sends the Follow out to swingout position on (1), gently sweeping the Follow past the Lead with the Lead's right arm, immediately releasing that arm, keeping the Follow's right hand in the Lead's left."

In addition to being a mouthful, this is unnecessarily confusing: is the Lead sending the Follow past his own body, or the body of a second Lead? And is he using his own arm, or the arm of a third Lead? As an experiment, we once tried teaching a whole class without pronouns, and everyone was much more confused than usual! Therefore, to make things clearer, we, like most teachers, use the pronouns "he" and "she" in our teaching. But in doing so, we feel it's important to clarify what we mean by them.

When we use the terms "he" and "she" in our teaching, whether in the classroom or on the page, we're not actually referring to human gender, but rather a form of grammatical gender.

In many languages other than English, it isn't only males that are masculine and females that are feminine. In fact, in Spanish, every noun has a gender: dance (*el baile*) is masculine, while music (*la música*), is feminine. Of course, Spanish speakers understand that dance isn't actually male and music isn't actually female: it's just that the structure of the language requires each noun to have a gender, so it does.

Similarly, we treat the word Lead as grammatically masculine, and the word Follow as grammatically feminine, referring to them as "he" and "she" respectively, regardless of the human gender of the dancers. (The same applies to our use of "him" and "her.") Our female Leads—of whom there are many and they're all amazing—understand that when we refer to their role as "he," we're not actually saying they're a man. Similarly, our male Follows—of whom there are also many and they're equally amazing—understand that when we refer to their role as "she," we're not actually saying they're a woman. The gender involved is only grammatical.

Demo Videos

Since dancing is four-dimensional (x, y, z, and time), it's often difficult to describe it perfectly in writing. For this reason, in addition to describing each of the 250+ variations in words, Nick and Melissa have created demo videos that allow you to see them all in action.

Next to the name of each variation described in this book, you'll see a three-letter code in brackets. For example, the code for the Swingout is SWO.

To see a video, go to crossstepwaltz.com/videos and enter the three-letter code in the box below the video. (You may want to bookmark this page, as you'll be returning to it often.) When you're ready to see the next video, simply enter the new code in the box.

If you want to see something more clearly, it's easy to slow down the video. Simply start the video and then click on the gear icon in the lower right corner of the video and select a slower "Playback Speed," e.g., 0.5 for half speed, or 0.25 for quarter speed.

As you play each video, we recommend that you watch what both roles are doing, rather than only watching your own role. Leads, it's important for you to know what the Follow is doing, so you can clearly lead her through it, and Follows, it's helpful for you to know both sides of the figure too, so you can help him through his part as well. (For more on this, see "Active Following" on p. 111 and "Empathetic Leading" on p. 129.)

Below each video, you'll find the option to enter another code and jump straight to that video.

Given how easy this is, we understand that it may be tempting to skip the reading and just watch the videos instead. But we strongly recommend against this. The written descriptions often include important details and tips that are easy to miss in a video, so it's essential that you read them as well as watching the videos.

Exceptions to the Rule

Of course, there are exceptions to almost every rule, so our suggestions for steps, variations, partnering, styling, and musicality will focus on what is generally true, most of the time. If we made a point, then stopped to explain every exception to that point, it would slow down your reading and distract from the main point. So if you ever find yourself thinking, "I can think of an exception," yes, so can we, but we want to make your reading experience as clear and efficient as possible.

Similarly, the videos of Nick and Melissa dancing each variation should be treated as just that: videos of one couple dancing each variation, not as a perfect model to be copied exactly in every detail. Everyone is different, so be prepared to adjust each variation as needed to make it comfortable for you and each of your partners.

Physical Practice

It's easy to sit on the couch, read a description, watch a video, and think "oh, I can totally do that!" It's quite another to actually do it. Therefore, instead of just being an "armchair dancer," we recommend that you get off the couch and dance the variations, to get them in your body as well as your mind. You can start to do this by yourself, "dancing with a ghost," so to speak, but in order to really understand the variations, you'll want to dance them with a partner.

Of course, just because you dance it once with a partner doesn't mean you'll actually remember it on the dance floor. Leads, it's easy to forget what you know in the heat of the moment, and Follows, you'll find that each real-world Lead will signal each variation in a slightly different way than your practice partner. Therefore, for both roles, your understanding of a variation won't be fully cemented until you dance it repeatedly with multiple partners.

If this sounds like a lot of work, don't worry: it's not actually as hard as it sounds. Dancing Cross-Step Waltz is supposed to be fun! And it is, as long as you approach it that way (for more on this, see "Work and Play" on p. 205). Therefore, rather than trying to master every one of the 250+ variations in one day, just try a few at a time. The Turning Basic and a handful of satisfying variations are all you really need to have a good time on the dance floor.

The Mindset

Although the variations included in this book are fun, they aren't the most important part of this book. Even if you can perfectly execute the footwork of every variation, it's possible that you still won't really be dancing Cross-Step Waltz. This is because Cross-Step Waltz is more than just a collection of moves. Even more importantly, Cross-Step Waltz is a mindset.

Therefore, in addition to describing the variations, we've also included a variety of essays—written by us and by our students—that shed light on this essential mindset. While knowing the steps is certainly important, it's in these essays where you'll really learn how to dance Cross-Step Waltz. To emphasize the equal importance of both aspects of the dance, we've interspersed the dance descriptions and essays throughout the book.

With these essential points of introduction out of the way, let's get right down to the dancing!

"On with the dance! Let joy be unconfined;
No sleep till morn, when youth and pleasure meet
To chase the glowing hours with flying feet."

— Lord Byron

Chapter 3

The Basics

Waltz Position

Cross-Step Waltz begins in waltz position, also known as closed position.

As illustrated below, the Lead's right arm is under the Follow's left arm, his right hand on her back and her left hand on his right shoulder. To accommodate the cross-steps, which pass through the frame, there may be a bit more space between the partners than in other dances, with the Lead's right hand on her left shoulder blade, rather than her spine.

His left hand and her right hand are palm-to-palm, lightly braced away from each other, with the Lead's fingers a bit more horizontal and the Follow's fingers a bit more vertical.

For a more detailed description of waltz position, with two pages of tips for making it comfortable, see our first book, *Waltzing: A Manual for Dancing and Living*.

Here's the basic footwork pattern that defines Cross-Step Waltz:

Basic Pattern of Cross-Step Waltz [BAS]

(1) The Lead crosses R over in front of L with weight, as the Follow crosses L over in front of R with weight.

(2) The Lead steps side L with weight as the Follow steps side R with weight.

(3) Both replace weight onto first foot (Lead's R, Follow's L), pulling that foot back slightly to make room for:

(4-5-6) Repeat opposite, crossing Lead's L and Follow's R over in front (4), stepping side with Lead's R and Follow's L (5), and replacing back onto Lead's L and Follow's R (6).

Throughout the step, your footwork should be the mirror image of your partner's.

Note: When dancing this with a partner, crossing "over in front" can also be thought of as crossing "through" the frame. Some dancers find it a bit easier to conceptualize this way.

The step on (1) is known as the primary cross-step. (4) is the secondary cross-step. A helpful hint is to shade (i.e., slightly turn) your body to face the direction you're crossing, rather than facing your partner squarely. This will make the cross-steps easier.

Leads: Be sure to allow your partner to shade her body back toward her secondary cross-step, toward the elbows side. Some Leads hold their partners so rigidly that their partners can't rotate their torsos into the second half. Rather than locking into a static frame, connect with your partner through a flexible frame, the shape of which you adapt moment-by-moment based on what is most comfortable for your partner.

Note: This non-turning version of Cross-Step Waltz is useful in order to understand the basic footwork and some of the fundamental dynamics of the dance. But while it's fundamental as *a* basic step, and appears in the dance as part of some variations, it isn't actually *the* basic step as it appears on the dance floor. That's the Turning Basic, which we'll describe next.

∞

Turning Basic [TRB]

This is the same footwork as above, but you do a full 360° turn with each set of six steps.

Begin in waltz position with the Lead facing the outside wall, held hands pointing along LOD. This starting orientation is essential for getting you traveling along LOD.

(1) The Lead crosses R over in front of L along LOD, while the Follow crosses L over in front of R along LOD (it feels like walking straight forward L).

Hints: Leads, your body is slightly ahead of her on this first step, as if crossing a finish line first. If you're not ahead of her, you'll have a difficult time passing into the outside lane on the second step. Follows, let him get ahead of you. If necessary, you can help him by gently sending him by with your left arm while taking a smaller step yourself.

(2) The Lead steps side/back around in front of the Follow with his L, his leg bridging over across LOD, while the Follow steps straight forward along LOD, with her R slightly between his feet. The Lead pulls himself backwards away from her on this step. Think "over the top" into the outside lane.

Hints: Make sure the Lead's L is actually fully across to the outside of LOD, not stepping on LOD. Imagine that his legs are a bridge and her right foot is a river: the bridge pylon that is his left leg should be fully across the river, on the opposite bank from where he started, i.e., in the outside lane. The Follow can help with this, if necessary, by sending him across to her right with her left arm. If he doesn't make it fully across, the Follow won't be able to step forward along LOD, and you'll both under-rotate, spiraling into the middle of the room. Follows, step straight forward into him, not swerving away to the right. Yes, it seems like he's a wall that's blocking you, but imagine you're a wizard on your way to Hogwarts, and confidently pass through the wall to Platform 9¾, intending to go straight through him along LOD.

(3) The Lead steps side R along LOD, while the Follow steps forward L along LOD. He pulls his right shoulder back out of her way into the outside lane, clearing a path so she's able to travel straight along LOD in the inside lane.

Hint: At this point, the couple has shifted their orientation, turning 180° while traveling along LOD. He's now in the outside lane, and she's now in the inside lane.

(4-5-6) The Lead does exactly what the Follow did, and vice-versa.

Follows: Your footwork can be thought of as "walk-2-3-4-pivot-pivot," walking straight along LOD for four counts, then flipping all the way around on the last two steps.

Leads: Look toward your right just before (4), to help direct your partner's travel along LOD. This is a visual lead, which is more comfortable than a physical lead pulling her in that direction. In other words, *let* her dance by on (4), instead of making her dance by.

The Turning Basic takes a little while to perfect, but once you have it, it flows effortlessly. It gets even better with practice.

General Hints: Every molecule of your body should be traveling (specifically, rolling CW) along LOD the whole time. Once you have the basic shape of things, morph even walking steps into the Turning Basic, to make it travel more smoothly. But keep these walking steps small: beginners tend to take very large steps to try to make it around their partner, who's also taking large steps, making it hard to get around. In particular, the person in the outside lane needs to take smaller steps to let the person in the inside lane get by. Once you're successfully traveling, think less about translating across the floor and more about rotating with your partner. Once the rotation is working, the translation will happen naturally.

Turning Basic (Waterfall Version) [WAT]

This is another version of the Turning Basic in which the Lead crosses behind on (4). It's commonly called "Waterfall."

Many Leads prefer Waterfall because it's physically easier to cross behind on (4), where there's more space, than to be constantly threading the needle under the elbows on (4). But other Leads prefer the perfect symmetry of the Turning Basic. It's entirely up to you: you can dance one, or the other, or a mix of both.

(1-2) The same as counts (1-2) of the Turning Basic.

(3) The Lead steps back along LOD with his right foot, while the Follow steps forward along LOD with her left foot. He pulls his right shoulder back out of her way.

Hint: As in the Turning Basic, at this point, the couple has shifted their orientation, turning 180° while traveling along LOD. He's now in the outside lane, and she's now in the inside lane.

(4) Instead of crossing L in front of R, the Lead crosses L *behind* R, as the Follow crosses R in front of L, as usual. Despite the difference in foot position for the Lead, the partnering should feel the same for the Follow, with the Lead "looking her by" into the second half.

(5-6) The same as counts (5-6) of the Turning Basic. Note that the Lead will need to turn even more than usual between (4) and (5), to go from crossing L behind to stepping straight forward along LOD between her feet, as usual.

For Leads, it will help to think, "forward-back-back, back-forward-forward." Follows, your steps are the same as before: "walk-2-3-4-pivot-pivot."

∞

Turning Basic vs. Waterfall

For the remainder of this book, whenever we write "Turning Basic," we mean either the original Turning Basic or the Waterfall version, as the Lead chooses. Just because it says "Turning Basic" doesn't mean that the Lead must cross in front on (4). Either version is fine. For variations where the Lead must cross in front or behind on (4), the Lead's foot placement will be clearly specified.

∞

Whichever version of the Turning Basic you prefer, we recommend starting a dance with some Turning Basics to connect with your partner before leading into other variations.

Starting with Sways [SWS]

Even before doing any basics, many dancers like to sway in place for a moment to establish a connection with their partner and synchronize with the music.

(1-2-3) Starting with *Lead's L and Follow's R* (not your usual Cross-Step Waltz foot), step side along LOD (1), then hold (2-3), swaying slightly along LOD.

(4-5-6) Replace side against LOD with Lead's R and Follow's L (4), then hold (5-6), swaying slightly against LOD.

Repeat, if desired, then:

(1-2-3) Same as (1-2-3) above.

(4-5) Replace side against LOD with Lead's R and Follow's L.

(6) Take weight on the forward foot, Lead's L and Follow's R, while the Lead begins to guide his partner into the primary cross-step of a Turning Basic on the next (1).

∞

Orbits [ORB]

You may have seen this one on *Dancing with the Stars*.

Stand side-by-side facing along LOD in half-closed position (letting go of the held hands, keeping the rear arms connected).

(1) Both step forward along LOD, with Lead's R and Follow's L. Keep your free hands floating around shoulder level, rather than letting them fall to your sides. (This isn't just a style pointer, it's important for the next step.)

Hint: The Lead is slightly ahead of the Follow, "winning the race," as in the Turning Basic.

(2) The Lead steps side/back around in front of the Follow with his L, as in the Turning Basic, but with his free left arm reaching across to catch her under her floating right arm. The Follow steps straight forward R between his feet, as in the Turning Basic.

(3) The Lead pulls his right shoulder back out of her way, letting go of right-to-left arms and stepping toward the outside wall with his R while the Follow steps forward along LOD with her L. At this point, the couple has switched places. He's now in the outside lane, and she's now in the inside lane, in half-closed position with the opposite arms (Lead's left under Follow's right).

(4-5-6) The Follow does exactly what the Lead did, and vice versa. The only difference is that her left arm reaches across to catch him *over* his right arm, rather than under it.

Leads: Don't toss her across too vigorously. She's a dancer, not a puppet, so let her dance across without hauling her. Lead clearly, but comfortably. For more on this, see "Empathetic Leading" on p. 129.

Follows: Translate this clear, comfortable lead at the micro scale into a large elegant movement at the macro scale. For more on this, see "Active Following" on p. 111.

Both: In this and other variations, visually track and adapt to your partner, rather than focusing only on your footwork.

This variation can also be done from closed position, as a **Lead's Fallaway** [LFA], holding the left-to-right hands the whole time. As the Lead tosses himself across to the outside lane, he opens up the elbows side to end up in open position holding left-to-right hands with the Lead on the outside lane. On the second half, he uses these hands to sweep the Follow across LOD in front of him.

∞

The Innovation [INN]

This is a Turning Basic without touching your partner. The name comes from Vernon and Irene Castle, who pioneered many of today's social dance conventions. They created a version of Tango in which they danced without touching, and called it the Innovation.

INNOVATION

While it's possible to dance it with your hands in your pockets or on your hips like the Castles, a safer arm position for dancing the Innovation in Cross-Step Waltz is to have your left arm floating above your partner's right arm, and your right arm floating below your partner's left arm. This makes it easy for either of you to catch your partner, if necessary.

While this may seem like an advanced concept, we've found that for both roles, when you're able to do a Turning Basic without touching your partner, helping your partner with your own body placement, your own dancing gets better. Then you can translate this improved body placement back into waltzing in closed position. So we use this advanced concept even when teaching beginners.

If you want to take this concept even further, see p. 187.

∞

Waltz Walk [WZW]

Sometimes, when traveling through a crowd, it's safer to walk forward in closed promenade position. When you're both facing forward, it's easier for you both to see and navigate together, and it also allows you to compress the frame in towards your partner in order to sneak through a smaller opening than you can dance a Turning Basic through.

The step itself is just walking forward for six steps, to two bars of waltz music.

To clearly signal this variation, the Lead takes a slightly firmer embrace, with his right arm reaching slightly farther around his partner and his left hand clearly "aiming" her forward.

While Waltz Walk is an easy and useful variation, there are few important things to keep in mind about it:

1. Waltz Walk isn't the basic of Cross-Step Waltz, only an occasional variation. Under normal conditions, the Turning Basic is the basic. Even for absolute beginners, the Turning Basic is easily accessible in a one-hour class, and it's much more satisfying than Waltz Walk.

2. When dancing Waltz Walk, it's essential that you keep stepping in time with the music, rather than slowing down or skipping steps. Take one step per beat, as always.

3. It's also essential to wait until (1) to re-enter the Turning Basic. While every other step of a Waltz Walk is a cross-step, it's only musical to re-enter the Turning Basic on the cross-step that falls on (1), not (3) or (5). For more on this, see "Musicality" on p. 69.

∞

Cross Swivels [CRS]

This is a stylized version of Waltz Walk.

(1) A non-rotating cross-step along LOD.

(2) A side step along LOD.

(3-4-5-6) Repeat, and repeat again, traveling six steps along LOD. The Lead must clearly lead each of the cross-steps, not just doing his own footwork.

As an optional styling, swivel slightly out away from your partner on (1), (3), and (5), and swivel slightly in towards your partner on (2), (4), and (6).

The Splits [SPL]

Sometimes, instead of a tight squeeze, there's an obstacle right in front of you.

In this case, you can temporarily split up from your partner, passing on either side of the obstacle, then rejoin each other after six counts for a Turning Basic. Give your partner a reassuring look, to let them know you're not abandoning them.

This can also be done as a bit of mischievous fun, leapfrogging another unsuspecting couple.

∞

Stop and Go [STG]

This variation temporarily stops the dance and starts it again three counts later.

(1) A non-rotating cross-step along LOD.

(2) The Lead stops his partner with a firmly planted side step along LOD.

(3) Hold, while starting to lead into another primary cross-step on (4).

(4-5-6) The start of a Turning Basic.

Note that the (4) of the music has now become the new (1) of the dance (and vice versa). As we'll discover later, this "phase-shifting" has many useful functions, like getting back on the downbeat when the song has an extra bar of music.

∞

Hesitating Side Sways [HES]

This takes the Sways from Starting with Sways and puts them in the middle of the dance.

(1) A non-rotating cross-step along LOD.

(2-3) The Lead stops his partner with a firmly planted side step (2), and hold (3), swaying a bit along LOD with feet apart.

(4-5) Shift weight to the rear foot, with feet still apart (4), and hold (5), swaying against LOD.

(6) Shift weight to the forward foot, ready to re-commence with a primary cross-step on the next (1).

This is particularly nice when you add a bit of Fred Astaire and Ginger Rogers' styling to it, drawing out an elegant figure eight with the sways: up and down along LOD on the first half, then up and down against LOD on the second half.

Chapter 4

No Contest

An essay by UT student Hyun Chang.

∞

I used to believe that anything involving physical activity was just impossible for me. But I didn't want to give up on anything entirely, considering that I only have a limited amount of time to explore my abilities and develop new ones. I came into social dance class thinking that I would just learn how to dance, and that would be it: this would just be another neat skill for me to learn. It wasn't until we began learning to waltz that dancing began to click for me.

Yes, I may not be great at physical activity, but in dancing I realized that the actual "dancing" portion was only 20% of the actual process. The rest was about learning: even though mistakes were made, there was no harm done. There was no competition, no race to become the best. Even in something as challenging as waltzing, as long as you enjoyed the dance and communicated to your partner that you were enjoying your time and were willing to work with them, that was all that mattered.

I started to understand that the whole reason I was so pessimistic about my abilities was because I was not enjoying them and because I used to think of them as a contest. Although I know I will not waltz all the time in my everyday life, I will keep this dance in the back of my mind for years to come to serve as an example of how enjoying the process—not turning the process into a contest—helped me accomplish something that I would have never dreamed of doing in a million years.

"I do not try to dance better than anyone else.
I only try to dance better than myself."

— Mikhail Baryshnikov

Chapter 5

Inside and Outside Turns

Many variations in Cross-Step Waltz are based on underarm turns for the Follow, so named because the Follow turns under the arms of the partners. Although there are many kinds of turns, they can generally be divided into two categories: inside turns and outside turns.

Inside and Outside Turns

To understand the difference between them, try the following exercise: take open two-hands with a partner, with the Follow's right hand in the Lead's left, and the Follow's left hand in the Lead's right. See that this two-handed connection forms a circle, or "frame," between you.

Take one of your two hand-to-hand connections and bring it *in* between you so that it passes through the center of the frame. A turn that starts this way is thus defined as an *inside* turn. Try it with the other hand: that's also an inside turn.

Now take one of your two hand-to-hand connections and bring it *out* away from the center of the frame. A turn that starts this way is thus defined as an *outside* turn. Try it with the other hand: that's also an outside turn.

Whether a turn is an inside or an outside turn is always defined from the perspective of the person who's turning. To understand why this is important, shake hands with a partner, taking a right-in-right handhold. Now take the Lead's hand and bring it across his body to the left. If the Follow turns under this hand, is it an inside turn or an outside turn? To the Lead, it feels like an inside turn, because his right hand is crossing in front of him. But to the Follow, it feels like an outside turn, because her right hand is going out away from her. Since the Follow is the one turning, it's defined the way she sees it: as an outside turn.

Similarly, if you take right-in-right hands and lead the Follow into a turn that starts by going out to the Lead's right side, it's defined as an inside turn because that's what it feels like for her, even though it feels like an outside turn to him.

If the Lead were the one turning under the hand, then (and only then) would the turn be defined by what it feels like for him.

Tips for Leading and Following Turns

Leads: The path of the hand is a circular "halo" around the Follow's head—not too high, not too low, just right for a halo. It's also important to make sure you keep your hand in front of her forehead, and never let it get behind her. Why? Because it's terribly uncomfortable—maybe even painful! If you don't believe it, have someone stand behind you and pull your arm back behind your head. Horrible, isn't it? You don't want to do that to your partner!

Just as it's important to lead the start of a turn, it's also important to lead the end of it. When she's done with the turn, bring your hand down to its regular position again. If you keep it high, she'll correctly interpret this as a signal that she should keep turning. On the other hand, if you're intending to lead multiple turns, keep the hand high and draw a second (or third) halo, as if "stirring a teacup." In any case, keep your hand in front of her at all times, tracking her rotation exactly, rather than trying to turn her faster or slower than she's able to.

Follows: "Noodle arms," which are loose and wiggly instead of firm and connected, can be a big problem in following turns. Here is a simple exercise that helps many Follows.

Face a partner without touching. Follows, raise your right arm straight in front of yourself, bending your elbow at a right angle, with your forearm raised vertically. Leads, use both of your hands to gently swivel the Follow's elbow (not her hand) back and forth to the left and right. Follows, make the connection of your upper arm (from shoulder to elbow) fairly firm, so that when your arm moves right or left, your body rotates CW or CCW along with it. When you feel pressure from your partner's hands on your elbow, apply equal and opposite "push-back pressure." Don't let your right elbow go off to either side.

For the second part of this exercise, raise the point of contact to the Follow's right hand. The Lead can use either hand to gently move the Follow's right hand a little to the left or right. Now the Follow is keeping her entire arm, all the way from shoulder to hand, firmly connected to her body. Once you're comfortable with that, the Lead can turn the Follow all the way around, CW or CCW, into an outside or inside turn.

At first, the Follow's right arm might feel a little stiff. But with practice, the Follow's right arm will become more relaxed, naturally responding with equal push-back pressure.

Keeping your arm firmly in front of you will also help save you if your partner accidentally turns you too fast or pulls your hand behind your head during a turn. In the first scenario, you can use your firm arm in front of you to signal how fast you can comfortably turn, and in the second, you can save yourself by "holding a pizza" with that hand, letting your fingertips point backwards over your head, while keeping your arm firmly in front of you. While your partner should know not to wrench your arm, you can also protect yourself.

Both: Hold each other's hands lightly during a turn, not clamping down on your partner's fingers. Your fingertips should swivel in your partner's like a universal joint. As an exercise to fix the clamping problem, try leading and following turns without touching, keeping the fingertips close together, without contact. Given that you can lead and follow a turn without touching, you definitely don't need to clamp. Instead, a light fingertip connection will do.

Free Spins, Rollaways, and Parallel Spins

In many cases, you can substitute a free spin, rollaway, or parallel spin for a Follow's underarm turn (either inside or outside).

In a free spin, the Follow spins solo next to the Lead, who is walking along beside her. To lead a free spin, lower the hands, and both brace into them with some push-back pressure. Then the Lead uses that pressure to lead the Follow to spin along beside him. In doing so, it's important to: (a) impart rotation, rather than just pushing her away, and (b) spin her in a specific direction (e.g., along LOD). It's also important to keep the hands low during a free spin, because if the hands begin to rise, the Follow might hold on, thinking it's an underarm turn.

In a rollaway, the Lead leads the Follow into free spin, then free spins himself, traveling next to her. In a rollaway, the Lead and Follow interact like interlocking gears, with one turning CW and the other turning CCW. Leads, make sure to lead her free spin first, rather than just spinning yourself, which would feel like you were ditching her. And make sure you keep up with her as she travels instead of just turning on the spot (Follows often have more experience with traveling turns than Leads do). Rollaways are led the same way as a free spin, with push-back pressure and a low-hand release. As an optional styling, while spinning, form an elegant curve with the arms that are leading the way (the right arm in a CW turn, or the left arm in a CCW turn), forearm slightly raised, parallel to the floor.

A parallel spin is like a rollaway, except that the Lead turns the same way as the Follow (i.e., CW when she's turning CW). Parallel spins are less common than rollaways, but when they work, they're a lot of fun.

While we've noted many of the best opportunities for these substitutions in the descriptions, we encourage you to experiment and discover even more!

∞

Follow's Turn Footwork

In most turns in Cross-Step Waltz, the Follow will be pivoting 180° per step along LOD. There are three different footwork techniques that Follows commonly use for turns:

- **Side Step Pivots**: Step side along LOD with one foot, then pivot 180° and step side along LOD with the other foot, keeping the feet under the body, slightly apart.

- **Forward-Back Pivots**: Step forward along LOD with one foot, then pivot 180° and step back along LOD with the other foot.

- **Châiné Turns**: A stronger step forward along LOD with one foot, then a smaller step back (almost in place) to complete the turn. This is often accompanied by "spotting," which means whipping your head around to see along LOD for as much for the rotation as possible. While this can be a pretty styling, it works best when you know in advance how many pivot steps you'll be taking, which isn't always the case in social dancing.

Some teachers over-specify the Follow's footwork for turns, saying that there is only one correct way for the Follow to pivot. While that may be true in a competition dance, Cross-Step Waltz is a social dance, so we respect the Follow's preferences.

One thing that doesn't work in Cross-Step Waltz is pirouetting on one foot on the spot, as some beginning Follows try to do. In Cross-Step Waltz, turns generally travel along LOD, and are taken one step per beat.

Of course, this all applies to Leads as well, when they're the ones turning.

∞

Waltz Walk Outside Turn [WWO]

This isn't the most exciting variation, but it's an easy way to practice one of the most common turns in Cross-Step Waltz: a Follow's outside turn on (4-5-6).

(1-2-3) Waltz Walk (p. 19).

(4-5-6) A Follow's outside turn CW. The Lead raises his left arm and the Follow steps forward R under it along LOD (4). Then the Follow pivots back L under the raised arms (5), and completes the turn by stepping forward R along LOD, as the raised arms are lowered and you return to waltz position (6).

∞

Double Outside Turn [DOT]

Once you've mastered the single outside turn, this double outside turn is even more fun.

After the cross-step on (1), the Lead sends the Follow into a double outside turn CW on (2-3-4-5). Note the delayed lead, waiting until (2) to lead the Follow under. This is because she needs her R free to step forward into a CW turn, and she doesn't have that foot free until (2).

The Follow pivots forward (2), back (3), forward (4), back (5) along LOD, as the Lead walks forward. Recover on (6) with a step along LOD, re-taking waltz position.

Follows: Often a Lead will accidentally try to turn the you under on (1)—a habit from Swing dancing—at which time you don't have the correct foot free for a turn. In this case, you can momentarily resist, delaying your turn to (2) and doing two turns to fill out the music. Follows tell us that when they do this with an inexperienced partner, he'll sometimes says, "Wow, that's the first time that actually worked!"

This could also be an **Outside Turn, Free Spin** [DOF], or an **Outside Turn, Rollaway** [DOR]. In both of these cases, the first turn (2-3) is led with a high hand, which is then brought down for a low-hand release into the Follow's free spin on (4). Her footwork is the same. In the Rollaway, his footwork on (4-5-6) mirrors hers, i.e., he pivots forward, back, forward along LOD, turning CCW while she turns CW.

Inside Turn with Grapevine Recovery [ITG]

(1) A non-rotating cross-step along LOD.

(2) The Lead rotates the Follow CCW and brings the held hands into the frame for an inside turn, as his right arm releases her. The Follow steps back R on (2), so the Lead must rotate her to face back against LOD just before she takes this step.

(3) The Follow steps side (or forward) L along LOD, with her back to him.

(4) Both step side along LOD, facing your partner.

(5) She crosses L behind, which is her natural inclination falling out of an inside turn. The Lead may either walk forward or cross behind (mirroring her).

(6) Both step side along LOD, retaking waltz position for a Turning Basic on (1).

Similar to the previous variation, this is a delayed turn, on (2). A common mistake is to bring the hands in on (1) before the CCW release on (2). On (1), the Follow is still facing forward, which means her right arm will wrap uncomfortably around her throat if the turn is led early.

With a low-hand release, this could also be an **Inside Free Spin with Grapevine Recovery** [IFG], or an **Inside Rollaway with Grapevine Recovery** [IRG]. In both of these cases, since the Follow will be navigating the beginning of the recovery alone, it's a good idea to lead an Inside Turn with Grapevine Recovery first, to practice the dynamic.

∞

Chained Inside and Outside Turns [CIO]

This goes directly from Inside to Outside Turns, every three steps.

(1-2-3) Lead a Follow's inside turn on (2) as above. Most dancers slip into open two-hands here, ending up with the Follow wrapped up in the right-to-left arms, and the left-to-right arms connected in front.

Leads: Make an extra effort to catch your partner's left hand with your right hand on (2), to take two hands. It's easy to let her left hand escape, and difficult to recover it once it does.

(4-5-6) An outside turn as in the Waltz Walk Outside Turn (p. 26). The Follow steps straight forward R along LOD into this turn (not facing him), so the Lead must use both hands to clearly lead her to face forward along LOD here, countering her natural inclination to face him.

(1-6) Repeat, if desired, then re-take waltz position after the outside turn when finished.

If the Follow already knows this figure, clearly leading it to her right hand alone will suffice, like waving a wand over her head. This is known as **Magic Wand** [MGW].

Double Inside Turn, Double Outside Turn [DID]

(1-6) He leads an inside turn on (2) but keeps his left hand raised, adding a little extra rotation to turn her under a second time. The Follow does traveling CCW pivots on (2-3-4-5-6). The Follow is backing on (6), so the Lead lowers the raised hand, with some push-back pressure, to clearly decelerate the Follow on (6).

(1) The Follow steps back L along LOD, bracing palms together to prepare for an outside turn.

(2-3-4-5-6) The Follow steps forward R along LOD into a Double Outside Turn (p. 26).

This could also be a **Double Inside Turn, Outside Turn and Free Spin**, or a **Double Inside Turn, Outside Turn and Rollaway**.

∞

Halo Frisbee [HAF]

For years, we've been using "halo" to describe outside turns, and "frisbee" for a free spin, but we credit Campbell Miller for putting them together in the nickname for this elegant figure.

This is the same as the previous figure but with a Follow's inside free spin on the first (4-5-6), then a Follow's outside free spin on the final (4-5-6). The Lead's left palm catches and braces against the Follow's right palm for the transition between the inside and outside turns.

Many dancers find it easier and clearer to brace right-to-right hands for the transition between the inside and outside turns because the Follow is at the Lead's right side and his right arm connects more directly to his core. This is known as **Halo Frisbee with R-in-R Hands** [HAH].

If you're feeling particularly adventurous, the free spins can be replaced with rollaways, for **Halo Rollaway** [HAR].

∞

Pivaloop

The Pivaloop, named by Andrea Reichart, isn't a full variation from closed position, but rather an element that can be satisfyingly combined with others, as described below. The Pivaloop itself starts with the partners side-by-side, facing LOD, with the Follow at the Lead's left side, holding inside hands (left-to-right).

Just before (1), the Lead swings the held hands downward and back against LOD, to lead the Follow to pivot CW in a diagonal path across in front of him, with his L hand continuing to loop over her head as she pivots. Her first Pivaloop step is a CW half turn, throwing her L shoulder and foot across LOD toward the outside lane (stepping side L looking back at him) on (1), so he must lead the downward pulse a moment early to rotate her into this backing step. Then she continues to pivot forward R, back L on (2-3).

Pivaloop Free Spin

After the Pivaloop, the Follow continues turning as the Lead leads her into a free spin, pivoting forward R, back L on (4-5). Catch your partner in waltz position on (6).

This could also be a **Pivaloop Double Outside Turn**, or a **Pivaloop Rollaway**.

∞

Cross-Body Inside Turn

This is a particularly nice way to get into position for a Pivaloop.

(1) Cross-step diagonally toward the center of the room, with the Lead sending the Follow forward past him.

(2-3-4-5-6) He leads her into a CCW inside turn across in front of him. End in open position, with the Follow in the inside lane, both facing forward along LOD, holding inside hands.

Note: The Follow completes two full rotations in these six counts (facing forward at the beginning, middle, and end of the turn), but only goes under the arm once.

∞

Cross-Body Inside Turn to Pivaloop Free Spin [CPF]

It's exactly that, two bars for each part. It has a satisfying dynamic of wind-up and unwind.

It could also be a **Cross-Body Inside Turn to Pivaloop Double Outside Turn** [CPT], or a **Cross-Body Inside Turn to Pivaloop Rollaway** [CPR].

∞

Pivaloop Around the World [PAW]

After (1-2-3) of a Pivaloop, the Lead quickly ducks forward under the arm on (4-5-6), passing in front of her to the outside lane, then leads another Pivaloop on (1-2-3) into a free spin on (4-5-6). As above, the free spin after the final Pivaloop could also be a turn or rollaway.

Leads: After you pass in front of her, circle her CW (like a do-si-do), to end up next to her before leading the second Pivaloop, rather than trying to lead it when she's behind you.

Cross-Body Triple Inside Turn [CBT]

For Follows who really like to turn, you can do a Cross-Body Triple Inside Turn, with the Follow stepping cross, back, forward, back, forward, back, forward, back, forward (1-9), pivoting diagonally across in front of the Lead and along LOD on the inside lane.

Note: The Follow completes four full rotations in these nine counts (facing forward five times including the beginning and end), but only goes under the arm three times.

Then sweep the Follow forward into the outside lane on (10-11-12). Note that this is a simple sweep across LOD, similar to the second half of Orbits (p. 17), not a Pivaloop.

∞

Arm Catch Free Spin [ACF]

This variation is from Lilli Ann and Claire Carey in Seattle.

(1-2-3-4) Turning Basic, letting go of the held hands on (4).

(5-6) As the Follow is backing across LOD, the Lead rolls her off his right arm, into the outside lane. She steps back, forward.

(1-2-3) That same Lead's right hand that guided the Follow away catches the Follow's left arm to lead a Follow's CCW free spin on (2-3). The most comfortable place to catch her arm will depend on how close you are to each other. She crosses in front, then steps back, forward.

(4-5-6) Catch left-to-right hands, and let the Follow do a Grapevine Recovery (p. 27).

∞

Free Spin Around the World [FPW]

This variation was invented by Tommy Anthony at UT Austin.

(1-2-3-4-5) Same as above.

(6-1-2) Rolling his right thumb down to maintain contact on the Follow's back with his palm, the Lead redirects her to walk CW behind his back to the inside lane, as he offers her his left hand at his left.

(3) The Follow takes his left hand with her free right hand.

(4-5-6) He sweeps her across LOD in front of him, similar to Orbits.

Throughout the second half, the Lead do-si-dos CW around the Follow to make it easier for her to orbit CW around him.

Chapter 6

How to Change Your Story

An essay by UT student Rissa Jackson.

∞

One amazing lesson I have learned through dancing is how fluid the concept of what I can and cannot do is. It might be a simple lesson, but it has changed my perspective immensely.

I thought I could not dance. However, we all more or less start out not knowing how to dance. It just takes time and energy to change that. Of course, classes can help cut down the time it might take, but the point is that many things can be changed if you want to change them.

Instead of being facts about myself, these might be more the stories I tell myself. I tell myself I cannot dance. I tell myself I am not artistic. I tell myself I am not flexible. But these are just stories, and I can change them all.

I can decide what to put my time and energy towards. I currently cannot play guitar, but I know I could learn how to play guitar if I truly wanted to. While that could be enjoyable, I do not currently feel the need to learn how to play guitar.

That is another powerful lesson. I can prioritize the things in my life that I really want to get better at. I don't have to stick with my story, but it's also not worthwhile to put my limited time and energy into changing everything.

These lessons are so freeing for me. I plan to spend some time over the break thinking about what my goals are and how to get there. I look forward to learning new things in the future, and continuing to change my story.

"Imagination is more important than knowledge.
Knowledge is limited.
Imagination encircles the world."

— Albert Einstein

Chapter 7

Lead Goes Variations

While most underarm turn variations in Cross-Step Waltz have the Follow going under, there's also a nice family of variations in which the Lead goes under (traditionally given the nickname "He Goes"). This puts you in open position with the Follow at the Lead's left. The advantage of this position is that you are closer to your partner while holding primary (left-to-right) hands, as opposed to when she's on his right, in which case he needs to reach over her with his left arm to guide her (or use the less common right-to-left hands).

∞

He Goes, She Goes [HGS]

(1-2-3) The Lead raises his left arm and travels straight forward under it, passing in front of the Follow to the outside lane, then lowers his arm, as the Follow crosses trails behind him.

(4-5-6) Both walk forward with the Follow in the inside lane. During these steps, the Lead rolls his left thumb down, so that his left palm is toward his partner.

(1-2-3) He raises his left hand and loops it in front of her head into a CCW Follow's inside turn, as she pivots forward, back, forward, staying in the inside lane.

(4-5-6) He lowers his left hand and sweeps her by in front of him to the outside lane and catches her in waltz position, as she crosses strongly forward across in front of him, then pulls her right shoulder back to let him get ahead of her for a Turning Basic on (1).

There are several essential hints to keep in mind for this variation, and those based on it:

- As the Lead goes under, he stays facing forward, passing to the outside lane, then leads her to walk forward next to him. If, instead, he turns to look back at her, he may mislead her into thinking they're going to travel against LOD.

- In addition, it's critically important that you don't omit the simple walking on (4-5-6). Although walking forward for three steps isn't the most interesting part of the variation, it's essential to wait until the Follow's L is ready for the CCW inside turn.
- Leads, you can help your partner get to your right side at the end by "crossing trails" behind her to the center of the room as she crosses in front of you toward the outside wall.

The inside turn on the third bar could also be a free spin, in which case it's **He Goes, Free Spin** [HGF], also known as "Frisbee." Or it could be **He Goes, Rollaway** [HGR].

∞

He Goes, She Goes with Waist Slide Ending [HGW]

This variation was created by Tyler Schattel at UT Austin.

On any of the above variations, the Lead does a waist slide on the final (4-5-6), raising his right elbow over the connected hands and spinning a full CCW rotation into his left arm, breaking through it, while he leads her in front of him to the outside lane. Note that you still exchange lanes during this waist slide, so that the Lead ends in the inside lane facing outward, and the Follow ends in the outside lane facing inward, ready to take waltz position.

∞

He Goes, She Goes with Grapevine Styling [HGG]

On the second bar of any He Goes, She Goes figure, do a mirrored grapevine, i.e., both cross in front (4), step side (5), and cross behind (6). Sometimes only the Follow does this grapevine. This has a nice wind-up feeling, before unwinding into the turn.

∞

He Goes, She Goes, She Goes, She Goes [HSR]

After the first three bars of any of He Goes, She Goes figure, repeat the second and third bars, one or more times, before moving on to final bar resolution. You can do the same turn each time, or vary it (maybe an Inside Turn, then a Free Spin, then a Rollaway).

This variation works best with clearly-led Grapevine Styling for the Follow on the bars between the turns.

∞

He Goes, Double Inside Turn, Pivaloop Double Outside Turn [HDI]

Leads often wonder what would happen if, instead of leading a second grapevine prep as above, they simply added a second turn to the Follow's inside turn on the third bar. While adding random turns to things usually doesn't work out cleanly, in this case, it does, by setting you up for a Pivaloop Double Turn exit.

(1-6) The first two bars of He Goes, She Goes.

(1-2-3) The usual inside turn with the Follow pivoting forward L, back R, forward L.

(4-5) A second inside turn with the Follow pivoting back R, forward L.

(6) The Follow steps forward R along LOD as the Lead begins to swing the connected hands down to sweep her into:

(1-6) A Pivaloop Double Outside Turn (p. 29).

If you're feeling particularly ambitious, the second turns can be replaced with free spins or rollaways, similar to Halo Frisbee or Halo Rollaway (p. 28).

In general, if the Follow is facing forward on the inside lane going into (4), you can exit with a simple sweep across LOD as in the fourth bar of He Goes, She Goes. And if the Follow is facing forward on the inside lane going into (1), you can exit with a Pivaloop Double Turn.

∞

He Goes, She Goes to Triple Outside Turn [HTT]

If you want a fancier way to exit out of He Goes, She Goes, or another figure that ends with a sweep across LOD on (4-5-6), try this:

(1-9) The first three bars of He Goes, She Goes.

(4) The Lead sweeps the Follow across the tracks into the outside lane.

(5-6-1) A Follow's outside turn, as she pivots back, forward, back.

(2-3-4-5) The Follow does two more outside turns, pivoting forward, back, forward, back.

(6) Recover with a step along LOD, taking waltz position.

This could also be **He Goes, She Goes to Double Outside Turn and Free Spin** or **He Goes, She Goes to Double Outside Turn and Rollaway.**

∞

He Goes, She Goes, Around the World and Free Spin [HAW]

Here's another fancy exit, invented by Danielle Baiata for the Waltz Lab (p. 165).

On the fourth and final bar of He Goes, She Goes, he places her right hand in his right and leads a right-in-right Pivaloop (p. 28) on (5-6), then slowly leads her behind his back (1-2-3-4-5-6), offering his left hand, putting himself in Hammerlock Position (p. 142). Then he leads a left-in-left Pivaloop (1-2-3) and Free Spin (4-5-6), sending her in front of him to the outside lane. Follows, continue orbiting around your partner the whole time.

∞

He Goes, Double Outside Turn [HGD]

This is an exception to the rule of not turning around to look back at her after he goes under.

The Lead ducks under his arm then turns halfway CW to walk backward along LOD, looking back at the Follow, while shifting back into the inside lane, for two bars. She walks straight forward, following his leading arm, the whole time. Once he's in the inside lane, it's a Follow's Double Outside Turn (p. 26) for her on the outside lane, starting on the next (2), for two bars.

This variation was invented by Nick and Melissa for a holiday class called "The 12 Days of Cross-Step Waltz." It was their interpretation of "11 Pipers Piping," with the Lead, the Pied Piper, leading the Follow along LOD.

As usual, this could also be **He Goes, Outside Turn and Free Spin** or **He Goes, Outside Turn and Rollaway**.

∞

Lead's Underarm Turn [LUT]

He Goes, She Goes requires a lot of space to travel, perhaps twenty feet or more. Sometimes the Lead begins He Goes, She Goes, then somebody cuts into the space ahead. The Lead's Underarm Turn is the perfect way to avoid a collision.

It's simply going immediately from the first bar to the fourth bar of He Goes, She Goes, i.e., He Goes (1-2-3), then sweep the Follow across in front to the outside lane (4-5-6).

Note: Despite the name, the Lead doesn't turn at all during this figure: he faces forward along LOD the whole time.

Hints: The Lead must cut into the outside lane quicker than in He Goes, She Goes, often backing slightly against LOD in the outside lane on (3), and he must bring his raised hand down sooner, to sweep the Follow past him on (4) with a low hand. The Follow quickly sees that this is a Lead's Underarm Turn, and cuts in front of him more dynamically than usual.

The Lead's Underarm Turn isn't necessarily an abandoned longer figure. It's often intentionally led, just for variety.

Waist Slide [WSL]

Instead of going under his left arm in the Lead's Underarm Turn, the Lead can break through that same arm as in a Waist Slide in Swing dancing.

The Lead's right arm passes over the left-to-right hands as the Follow's right arm slides across (or passes near) his waist. Then the left-to-right arms stay connected just long enough to wrap her around him to make it clear that she's passing in front of him to the outside lane on the second half.

Unlike the Waist Slide in He Goes, She Goes with Waist Slide Ending (p. 34), in this version, the Lead doesn't turn at all: he simply faces forward the whole time.

If the Lead keeps his right arm down and places the Follow's right hand on his right shoulder, allowing it to slide across his shoulders instead of his waist, it becomes a **Shoulder Slide** [SSL].

"You can make more friends in a month by becoming interested in other people than you can in a year by trying to get other people interested in you."

— Dale Carnegie

Chapter 8

Connection

Social dancers and dance teachers alike emphasize the importance of connection in partnering. There are two kinds of connection—physical and mental. Some teachers stop after working on the physical connection, but we think both forms of connection are essential.

The Physical Connection

Connection is how dancing feels to you and your partner, not how it looks.

In order to communicate with your partner, you need to have a physical connection that is balanced and reciprocal, with the Lead and Follow contributing equally.

When you and your partner are in closed position, hold each other with comfortably braced hands, without clamping, and somewhat firm arms, without being rigid. Translate the movement of your body through your arms to your hands, and vice versa.

In open position, when holding one or both hands, comfortably push or pull back on your partner's hands, providing equal and opposite pushback or pullback pressure. While you still want to avoid rigidity, you also want to avoid limp "noodle arms."

When pulling, imagine you're water-skiing, allowing the pull you feel in your hands to translate through your arms to move your whole body, and vice versa. When pushing, imagine you're pushing the boat away from the dock, using your whole body to push through your arms to your hands, and vice versa.

In the beginning, you may find that it takes a moment for these physical signals to travel through your body, as you think "oh, my hand's moving, I should probably go with it." But eventually, as you discover what this kind of connection feels like, the process of leading and following will become increasingly natural, until it's as if you're moving as one.

The Mental Connection

While physical connection is essential, the best dance partners, both Lead and Follow, understand that there's more to it than that. The mental aspect of connection is just as important.

Three essential aspects of mental connection are:

- Your partner is a living, caring person with feelings. Treat your partner with kindness, consideration, and your full attention.

- The best form of mental connection is empathy. Empathy is as simple as having an awareness of how your dancing feels to your partner. The goal of this empathetic connection is to improve your partner's dance experience, through clearer and more comfortable leading, more compassionate following, or a reassuring smile.

- Connection is a two-way conversation. Just as Follows are aware of and responsive to the Lead's choices, Leads are aware of and responsive to the Follow's choices. Both roles constantly adapt and adjust to each other with balanced reciprocity. Everyone dances; no one gets danced. In the end, when you help your partner have fun, you will also have more fun.

∞

In the words of Stanford student Valeria Wu:

> I used to think that being a good dancer meant that you could easily follow people who danced really well. Then I learned that those who are true dancers are those who can have fun with someone who doesn't know how to dance at all. Laughing at every misstep, getting back on the beat, and smiling at your partner to make them feel confident, are skills that can take you very far in life. The fundamental idea of putting yourself in someone else's shoes and empathizing is crucial for life. After all, knowledge can only take you so far—it's the meaningful connections you create with people that truly makes the difference.

Chapter 9

Empathy

An essay by Stanford student Julia Quintero.

∞

I've spent a lot of time this quarter thinking about empathy. Empathy asks us to get out of our heads and into someone else's. It asks us to see the world through a lens that is not our own.

Social dance asks us to keep a nimble mind that is always attuned to our partner. That alone is an exercise in empathy. In fact, our sense of empathy must be so sharp that we can understand someone not through words, but through subtle body movements—a shift of weight, a knowing look exchanged. Not only are we learning to tune in via body language, we are also doing so in a matter of seconds, in real-time—reading and reacting in a constant loop of empathic effort. In doing so, empathy asks us to understand, rather than to judge, our partner.

As one of the least experienced dancers in the intermediate class, I experienced a range of empathic responses from various partners—some of whom would impatiently react to my mistakes and mishaps with disapproving looks or frustrated grimaces, while others would smile and kindly guide me towards the right steps and turns. I feared the former; I thrived with the latter. I will always be grateful for the partners who took the effort to extend empathy towards me—to remember what it was like when they were first learning, to tune into the nervousness in my movements and to calm me with reassuring smiles.

I am also grateful for the partners who may have been less-than-empathetic towards me. I'd like to think it was my own empathic challenge, a unique opportunity to practice understanding towards a non-understanding person. "Okay, why might this person be frustrated? What does this experience feel like for him?" I'd like to believe that it sharpened my ability to take perspective and tune into my partner's beliefs, desires, knowledge, percepts, thoughts, feelings, and intentions. In this way, social dance has helped me to become not only a better dancer, but also a better person.

"Self-absorption kills empathy.
When we focus on ourselves,
our world contracts as our problems loom large.
But when we focus on others, our world expands."

— Daniel Goleman

Chapter 10

Grapevine Variations

This is one of the most important families of Cross-Step Waltz variations. A grapevine makes traveling laterally easier than taking side-close steps and more interesting than simply walking. The alternation of cross-steps in front and behind also sets the Follow up for a variety of turns.

If you haven't danced a grapevine before, here's the basic concept:

The Grapevine

Without a partner: (1) Cross a foot (either one) over in front of the other foot. (2) Take a side step. (3) Cross behind. (4) Take another side step. Repeat.

Or you might begin by crossing behind on (1), then crossing over in front on (3).

∞

With a partner, there are two different kinds of Grapevine you can do:

The Parallel Grapevine

(1) The Lead crosses behind as the Follow crosses in front. (2) Side step along LOD. (3) He crosses in front as she crosses behind. (4) Side step. Repeat.

∞

The Mirrored Grapevine

(1) The Lead crosses in front as the Follow also crosses in front. (2) Side step along LOD. (3) He crosses behind as she also crosses behind. (4) Side step. Repeat.

While some variations, such as He Goes, She Goes with Grapevine Styling (p. 34), use this mirrored grapevine footwork, in this chapter, most grapevines will be parallel grapevines.

In a waltz, there are three counts, not four, so the two most common types of grapevine in Cross-Step Waltz are the Three-Count Grapevine and the Six-Count Grapevine.

The Three-Count Grapevine

(1) The Lead crosses R behind as the Follow crosses L in front. (2) Side step along LOD. (3) He crosses R in front as she crosses L behind.

The Six-Count Grapevine

(1) The Lead crosses R behind as the Follow crosses L in front. (2) Side step along LOD. (3) He crosses R in front as she crosses L behind. (4) Side step. (5) The Lead crosses R behind as the Follow crosses L in front. (6) Side step.

Tips for Leading and Following Grapevines

Leads: You're used to crossing in front on (1), so it may take a conscious effort to remember to cross behind on (1). If you miss your cross behind on (1), you can either bail on the grapevine and do something else while you regroup to try again, or you can clearly lead the Follow through her part of the grapevine while you just walk beside her along LOD.

To clearly lead a parallel grapevine, move your shoulders in concert with the crossing feet, pulling your right shoulder back to lead her to cross in front when you're crossing R behind, and pushing it forward to lead her to cross behind when you're crossing R in front.

Follows: Stay connected throughout your whole body, from your shoulders to your feet. This is as opposed to allowing your body to become disconnected at the waist. Movement in your shoulders should be seamlessly translated into movement in your feet. Specifically, if your left shoulder is pulled forward, let that also pull your L forward to cross in front. If your left shoulder is pushed back, let that also push your L back to cross behind.

Grapevine Outside Turn [GOT]

(1-2-3) A Three-Count Grapevine: Lead crosses R behind as the Follow crosses L in front (1), side step along LOD (2), Lead crosses R in front as the Follow crosses L behind (3).

(4-5-6) A Follow's CW outside turn on the outside lane: both step along LOD letting the Follow face forward along LOD (4), then the Follow pivots back (5), forward (6) under the arm as the Lead walks forward along LOD.

Many dancers prefer the connection of an optional tuck on (3), bracing left-to-right hands. The Follow is falling back at this time, rotating CCW, which naturally brings her right arm forward into a braced tuck.

This could also be a **Grapevine Free Spin** [GFS]. But the problem with leading a free spin from closed position is that there's no rising arm to warn the Follow that a turn is about to happen, so the Follow's left hand can sometimes get caught on the Lead's right shoulder. Leads, it's your responsibility to make sure the Follow's left hand doesn't get caught on your back. You can do this by lowering your shoulder and arm out of the way of her arm, rather than expecting her to lift her arm in time.

∞

Two-Hand Grapevine Free Spin [TGF]

A better solution to that problem is to slip out to open two-hands for a Grapevine Free Spin, perhaps at the end of the previous Turning Basic.

This also enables a variety of other grapevine turns, including:

- **Two-Hand Grapevine Rollaway** [TGR]: A rollaway on (4-5-6).

- **Two-Hand Grapevine Parallel Spin** [TGP]: A parallel spin on (4-5-6), i.e., the Lead spins CW as the Follow spins CW.

- **Two-Hand Grapevine Outside Turn** [TGO]: The rear hand can help send the Follow under the forward hands.

- **Two-Hand Grapevine Inside Turn** [TGI]: If the Follow turns under the rear hands instead, that makes it an inside turn.

∞

Rear-Hand Grapevine Free Spin

Some figures end with holding only your partner's rear hand. From this right-to-left handhold, the Lead can lead a one-handed Grapevine Free Spin. (Or Inside Turn, or Rollaway.)

In this case, the Lead often doesn't do the grapevine himself, he just leads it for the Follow. (Or he might do a mirrored grapevine.)

For example, try a **Waist Slide to Rear-Hand Grapevine Free Spin** [WSF]. After the Waist Slide, take rear hands for a Grapevine Free Spin. It's a nice, swoopy combination.

∞

Rear-Hand Face Loop [RHF]

Another way to resolve holding rear hands is to lead a rear-hand face loop straight into a Turning Basic. The Lead takes left-to-right hands and drifts in front of the Follow for a Turning

Basic on (1), while looping the right-to-left hands over the left side of his head, with his right arm in front of his face and her left arm behind his head, dropping it on his right shoulder to take waltz position. It takes a bit of practice to get it the first time, but once you do, it quickly becomes second nature.

∞

Chained Grapevine Turns [CGT]

(1-6) Start with a Grapevine Outside Turn (from closed position or two hands).

After the Follow's CW turn on (4-5-6), the Follow is ready to cross in front again on (1). Therefore, another grapevine turn can be done right after that, or perhaps several grapevine turns in a row. It's easy and fun to change the kind of CW turn each time, from an outside turn the first (4-5-6), to an inside turn the next (4-5-6), or a free spin, rollaway, or parallel spin.

∞

Dishrag

Dishrag is a nickname for a Follow's underarm turn under both hands, led from open two-hands. The terms inside and outside turn are no longer relevant in Dishrag turns, but if the Lead is aware that inside turns are more comfortable to follow than outside turns, he will apply a bit more pressure with his right hand, and correspondingly less pressure with his left.

Hint: Don't let your wrists cross, or else this will lock up. But also avoid letting the arms separate, as this will uncomfortably pull the Follow in two different directions. Instead, keep all of the fingertips in one point that circles the Follow's head like a halo.

After a Dishrag, the hands end up crossed.

∞

Grapevine Dishrag, Grapevine Free Spin [GDR]

It's just that. Since the hands end up crossed after Dishrag, a free spin is a natural resolution.

∞

Inside and Outside Grapevine Combinations [IOG]

Begin with He Goes, She Goes, She Goes, She Goes (p. 34), which is a combination of grapevines and turns with the Follow on the inside lane. Chain together any number and kind of turns.

Then exit as usual, with the Follow sweeping across the tracks into the outside lane on any (4-5-6), except instead of taking waltz position, the Lead offers open two-hands. Then he leads Chained Grapevine Turns (p. 46), which is a combination of grapevines and turns with the Follow on the outside lane. Chain together any number and kind of turns.

Six-Count Grapevine, Double Outside Turn [SCG]

This is one of the most popular Cross-Step Waltz figures.

If you do a long grapevine for two bars of music (six steps), the Follow will be crossing behind on the next (1). That can be a preparatory tuck before an outside turn. Since the next phrase of music is two bars, there's time for a double outside turn on (2-3-4-5-6).

Leads, don't forget to delay the Follow's outside turn until (2). Tuck on (1), turn on (2).

This could also be a **Six-Count Grapevine, Outside Turn and Free Spin** [SCF] or a **Six-Count Grapevine, Outside Turn and Rollaway** [SCR].

∞

Five-Count Grapevine, Inside Turn and Outside Turn [FIO]

This was invented by Googlers Mark Zavislak and Chen Zheng in the Waltz Lab (p. 165).

(1-5) Five counts of a six-count grapevine. On (5), the Follow is crossing in front.

(6-1-2) A Follow's CCW inside turn, pivoting back, forward, back.

(3) The Lead stops her CCW rotation by bracing palms together in a tuck, as the Follow takes another step back along LOD.

(4-5-6) He leads her into an outside turn, the Follow pivoting forward (4), back (5), then catch each other in waltz position with a step along LOD (6).

∞

Twelve-Count Grapevine [TCG]

If you accidentally do more than six steps of a grapevine, you can continue for another six, exiting after a total of twelve grapevine steps.

The good news is that the Follow will be ready to cross in front when you're finished, so she can exit to a Turning Basic on (1). The Lead will cross in front twice in a row, on (11) and (1).

But twelve steps of a grapevine is almost a bit too much. For a way to make it more interesting, see the Tango-inspired Grapevine Rueda (p. 63).

∞

Co-Waterfall [CWF]

If you accidentally exit to a Turning Basic after six counts of a grapevine, the Follow will be crossing behind. But that's alright: you'll simply be doing Co-Waterfall.

Co-Waterfall is a Turning Basic in which both the Lead and Follow do the Lead's Waterfall footwork, as danced by Ryan Gosling and Emma Stone in the film *La La Land*.

Lead's (1-2-3): The same steps as in Waterfall.

Follow's (1-2-3): The same as the Lead's (4-5-6) in Waterfall, beginning by crossing L behind R, in the outside lane.

(4-5-6) Each does what their partner did on (1-2-3).

In other words, whoever is on the inside lane is crossing in front, and whoever is on the outside lane is crossing behind.

The whole step is danced with your partner to your right side, right hip to right hip.

After six counts of a Grapevine, you can do one Co-Waterfall, then lead back into a normal Turning Basic. Or see what you can invent from a longer series of Co-Waterfalls.

∞

Waterfall Grapevine

(1-2-3) The first half of Waterfall.

(4-5-6) The fourth step of Waterfall (Lead crossing L behind, Follow crossing R in front) begins a grapevine that travels laterally along LOD, "toward the elbows" with the Lead in the outside lane and the Follow on the inside lane. The Follow grapevines by crossing R in front (4), stepping side L (5), and crossing R behind L (6), as the Lead crosses L behind (4), steps side R (5), and crosses L in front (6).

The Follow crossing behind on (6) winds up for some nice unwinding figures.

Leads: Lead this even more clearly than a normal grapevine, as it can come as a bit of a surprise. Really roll your shoulders forward and back, so that you're side-by-side, right hip to right hip on (4), and left hip to left hip on (6).

∞

Waterfall Grapevine Inside Turn [WGI]

(1-2-3) The first half of Waterfall.

(4-5-6) Waterfall Grapevine, traveling along LOD.

(1-2-3) A Follow's inside turn as in He Goes, She Goes (p. 33), releasing the elbows-side connection, which is now pointed along LOD, blossoming forward along LOD into this turn.

Leads, make sure your partner is facing forward along LOD, with your right arm completely released, on (1).

(4-5-6) He sweeps her across LOD in front of him, as in He Goes, She Goes, closing up to waltz position.

As the second half of this is the same as the second half of He Goes, She Goes, anything that modifies or comes out of the second half of He Goes, She Goes can modify or come out of a Waterfall Grapevine Inside Turn.

For example, try a **Waterfall Grapevine Inside Turn with Waist Slide Ending** (p. 34), or a **Waterfall Grapevine Inside Turn to Triple Outside Turn** (p. 35).

∞

Long Waterfall Grapevine, Slow Outside Turn [WGO]

(1-6) Waterfall Grapevine.

(1-2) Add two more grapevine steps.

(3-4-5-6) A slow outside turn for the Follow. The Lead sends the Follow into the outside lane during the outside turn, as he travels behind her into the inside lane. It feels like he's orbiting CW around her.

∞

Pivoting Five-Count Grapevine

This family of variations evolved during the Waltz Lab (p. 165), from a seed of an idea by Susan de Guardiola in New Haven, CT, taken further by Nick and Melissa, using elements that Richard had developed. Teamwork!

Here's the basic concept:

(1-2-3) Three steps of grapevine, starting with the Lead crossing behind and the Follow crossing in front.

(4-5) A half pivot, Lead backing around on (4), then a side step along LOD on (5).

(6-7-8) Three steps of grapevine, starting with the Lead crossing in front and the Follow crossing behind.

(9-10) A half pivot, Follow backing around on (9), then a side step along LOD on (10).

Note that the second five counts are role-reversed, with the Follow doing exactly what the Lead did, and vice-versa.

There are several ways of musically incorporating this sequence into Cross-Step Waltz:

Doubled Pivoting Five-Count Grapevine [PFG]

Do that ten-count sequence twice, then resolve it with four more counts of grapevine. The Follow's grapevine leads straight into her primary cross-step, while the Lead needs to cross in front twice in a row at the end, on (23) and (1).

If the timing seems unmusical, with these five counts against the waltz music, the secret is to count down on the timing of the pivot step. The first pivot happens on (4), then (3), then (2), then (1), i.e., 1 2 3 **4** 5 6 / 1 2 **3** 4 5 6 / 1 **2** 3 4 5 6 / **1** 2 3 4 5 6.

∞

Pivoting Five-Count Grapevine, Double Outside Turn [PFD]

If you only want to do one Pivoting Five-Count Grapevine, you can resolve it with a double turn as in the Six-Count Grapevine, Double Outside Turn (p. 47).

Start with one full ten-count cycle of Pivoting Grapevine, then dance:

(11-12-13) Three steps of grapevine, starting with the Lead crossing behind and the Follow crossing in front. On (13), which is a musical (1), the Follow is crossing behind, so this is a good time to tuck.

(14-15-16-17-18) A Follow's double outside turn.

This could also be a **Pivoting Five-Count Grapevine, Outside Turn and Free Spin** or a **Pivoting Five-Count Grapevine, Outside Turn and Rollaway**.

∞

Hesitating Five-Step Grapevine [HFG]

The latest evolution of the Five-Count Grapevine happened at the 2019 Waltz Weekend in Berea, KY, where it was discovered that it works even better if you do the five steps in six counts. This allows the symmetrical ten-step sequence be danced once through as a perfectly-encapsulated twelve-count figure.

Dance the Five-Count Grapevine described above, but hold the pivots for two counts (4-5), then fall into the fifth step (a side step) on (6). This way, you'll be right back where you started after twelve counts, so you can exit to a Turning Basic, or repeat it, if desired. If you pivot higher on the ball of the foot on (4-5), it feels wonderfully light and swoopy.

Nine-Count Orbiting Grapevine Turns [NCG]

(1-5) A regular five-count grapevine (non-pivoting), beginning with the Lead crossing behind and the Follow crossing in front.

(6-7-8) He leads her into a cross-body inside turn, releasing his right arm as she turns in and under. As she turns, the Lead orbits with her, passing behind her into the outside lane.

(9) Recover with a side step along LOD, taking open two-hands.

(1-5) A five-count grapevine with two hands, again beginning with the Lead crossing behind and the Follow crossing in front, but this time with the opposite foot in the opposite lane.

(6-7-8) A Follow's outside turn, sending her in front of him to the outside lane. Again, the Lead orbits with her, passing behind her into the inside lane.

(9) Recover with a step along LOD, taking waltz position.

Technically, the counts of the second half are (4-5-6-1-2-3-4-5-6), but it's easier to parse (both in a description, and on the dance floor) when you count it as two sets of nine.

∞

Matador

Matador is an open two-hand outside turn in which the Follow's left hand is low behind her back as she turns under her raised right arm. To get into it, take open two-hands and turn the Follow CW under the arch of her raised right arm, while her left hand is lowered to a position behind her back.

Open two-hand figures can go toward either side, and either the Follow or Lead can go under. This means that there are three other Matador options, turning the Follow CCW toward the other side, or the Lead can go under either arch.

The name "Matador" is from the disco era. This position is also called Hammerlock, but we like the specificity of the term Matador because the term Hammerlock is applied to a variety of other different positions.

Hammerlock is a wrestling move, and is thus supposed to hurt, with the victim's arm forced upward behind their back. We don't want this to hurt, so it's important to keep the Follow's left hand comfortably low behind her back. Follows, you can actively help with this, protecting your own arm by placing it where it's most comfortable behind your back.

If you get stuck on the way in, with the elbows of the high arms awkwardly hung up on the low arms, the key is to keep the high arms high and keep turning until you're fully facing your partner and the high arms have passed completely over the low ones.

Two-Hand Grapevine, Matador Around the World [GMA]

(1-2-3) A two-hand grapevine.

(4-5-6) A Follow's outside turn along LOD, but keeping the rear hands held low. Those hands end up comfortably low behind the Follow's back.

(1-2-3) Using both hands, the Lead guides the Follow to walk CW behind his back to the inside lane, as he stays facing forward.

(4-5-6) Using only the left-to-right hands, the Lead sweeps the Follow across the tracks into the outside lane.

∞

Two-Hand Grapevine, Matador Wheel [GMW]

Starts and ends the same as above, but once in Matador, wheel CW around each other for two bars, both walking forward, completing one full rotation on the spot, before doing the Around the World exit.

∞

Grapevine Outside Turn to Inside Turn and Outside Turn [OIO]

(1-2-3) The usual grapevine in closed position, with the Lead crossing behind on (1).

(4-5-6) A Follow's outside turn along LOD, but this time the Lead plants himself in swingout position and firmly stops the Follow in a rock step back on her R on (6), as he rocks back L. Rather than completing a full turn as usual, the Follow only rotates halfway CW, facing against LOD at the end of this bar.

(1-2-3) Rewind with an inside turn, the Follow traveling against LOD and the Lead stopping her with a shoulder catch with his right hand when she's rocking back L, facing along LOD. (Leads, if she's reaching for waltz position, you can catch her forearm instead of her shoulder.)

(4-5-6) A Follow's outside turn along LOD, with the Lead traveling forward along LOD with her. The Lead is standing in place during the Outside and Inside Turns, so to get restarted on the final bar, he steps forward L on (4).

This can also conclude with a Follow's Free Spin on (4-5-6).

In this variation, the Follow is dancing Three-Step Swing, a step which is commonly seen as part of a variety of vernacular dances around the world, including Venezuelan Merengue and South African Sokkie. It's similar to the regular four-step swing (step, step, rock-step), but with one less step (step, rock-step), meaning that you do your rock-step on alternating feet, rather than rocking on the same foot each time.

General Guidelines for Constructing Grapevine Variations

While this chapter includes detailed descriptions of the best grapevine figures from the past two-and-a-half decades of innovation in Cross-Step Waltz, it's also helpful for dancers of both roles to understand the basic theory behind how grapevine variations are constructed. This will not only help you create your own (p. 165): it will also help you understand how to lead and follow any grapevine variation more comfortably.

Every two steps of a grapevine, the Follow is either turning CW or CCW. This means that she can turn more CW or CCW at these times, into an underarm turn or a free spin. Leads, always lead the Follow to rotate more in the direction she's already rotating, rather than fighting her existing rotation.

Specifically, during a standard Six-Count Grapevine, the Follow is set up to step back along LOD into a CCW turn on (2), forward into a CW turn on (4), back into a CCW turn on (6), or forward into a CW turn on the next (2).

Count	1	2	3	4	5	6	1	2
Follow Can Turn	-	CCW	-	CW	-	CCW	-	CW

Leads, watch your partner closely, for the perfect split-second to send your partner into a turn from a grapevine. Don't just count the number of steps that are in the written description. Your partner can tell if you're aware of her smooth rotational flow from a grapevine into the turn, or if you're just counting steps (or worse, neither).

It's also useful to know that coming out of a CW turn, the Follow will naturally be set up to cross L in front. Coming out of a CCW turn, the Follow will naturally be set up to cross L behind. This is important in order to determine what can comfortably come next.

If the grapevine starts in a different way (e.g., a Waterfall Grapevine), the letter of the law won't apply anymore, but the spirit certainly will. The counts on which the Follow can turn each direction will be different, as will the feet she's crossing with, but the bottom line is the same: look for the times when she's already turning, and turn her more the same way.

"It is with your feet that you move,
but with your heart that you dance."

— Anonymous

Chapter 11

Avoiding Boredom

Adapted with permission from an essay by Tango dancer Veronica Toumanova, originally published in her book *Why Tango*.

∞

We often hear Leads complain: "When I dance, I get bored with my own dancing. At some point it seems like I have already danced all the combinations, tried all the variations, and I just don't have any inspiration anymore. It's a terrible feeling because if I'm bored with myself, the Follow must be bored out of her mind with me."

There exists a myth among Leads that to give a Follow "a good time" you need to know a large amount of steps. But most of the time, the Follow is way too busy dancing to keep score of what steps the Lead has used, or hasn't.

Besides, it's not the vocabulary that the Follow finds attractive in a good Lead, but the deliciousness of her own movement in response to his lead. Too few variations is never the reason a Follow becomes bored—what makes her check out is the absence of connection.

This may be because the Lead dances in an automatic and unconscious way, devoid of feeling, or because he is too preoccupied with his own steps and forgets about her.

As a Lead, you could be a dance encyclopedia and bore your Follow out of her mind, or have only some simple elements in your vocabulary and make her melt in your arms. The value is never in the quantity, but in the quality.

So if it isn't a lack of steps that leads to boredom, what is it?

Dancers get bored with themselves for the same reason we get bored with any activity, no matter how complex it is: it has to do with the feeling of routine. Routine sets in not only because you repeat the same things over and over again, but also because you repeat how you do them again and again. Routine is when you become predictable to yourself, when your reality stops being surprising and delightful to you.

So how best to deal with your boredom in dancing?

One solution is to combine or modify steps you already know, changing the order of the elements, or the timing, or the ending. But there is also a deeper, more important level on which you can deal with the sensation of boredom.

It is about switching your focus from what you do to how you do it.

The next time you feel bored, start consciously directing all of your attention to how you move in that particular moment and try to grasp the fullness of the sensations available to you: from yourself, from your partner, from your environment, from the music. Your boredom will cease to exist in the instant you put your full attention on the unique circumstances of the present moment, which has never happened exactly like this before, and will never happen exactly like this again.

> "I've learned that
> people will forget what you said,
> people will forget what you did,
> but people will never forget
> how you made them feel."
>
> — Maya Angelou

Chapter 12

Variations Inspired by Tango

Cross-Step Waltz and Tango share many similarities. In fact, in *The Tango and How to Dance It* (1913), Gladys Crozier described a "Tango Waltz Figure" that was essentially a Cross-Step Waltz Turning Basic in slow 4/4 timing. In addition, the shape of the Ochos in early Tango was essentially a non-turning Cross-Step Waltz step. In honor of these and other similarities, here are some Tango-inspired variations of Cross-Step Waltz.

∞

Follow's Solo [FSO]

(1) The Lead takes his primary cross-step and completely stops, as the Follow begins a non-turning basic (p. 14).

(2-3) The Follow finishes the first half of a basic in place, as the Lead remains in place.

(4-5-6) With a CCW rotation of the frame, he leads the Follow to return to place with the second half of a basic. His weight can shift forward and back in place as he leads her back and forth beside him.

Three common problems for Leads to avoid:

- If you stop yourself before you take your primary cross-step on (1), you won't have a stable stance from which to lead your partner. So take the cross-step.

- Don't just stop your footwork, with a dead frame. Your partner will think she's supposed to stop as well, and will. Instead, use your frame to continue leading your partner forward into the first half of a basic (it feels like a slightly pushing lead), and then forward into the second half (it feels like a slightly pulling lead).

- Since you have your weight on your crossed R during the Follow's Solo, a possible mistake is for you to try to recommence a Turning Basic on your L. Instead, shift back onto your L on (6), without weight on your R, then re-step on your crossed R on (1).

Another option is for the Lead to stop on a side step along LOD on (2). This **Lead's A-Frame Stance in Follow's Solo** [FSA] is a common position from which similar figures are led in modern Argentine Tango.

∞

In a Follow's Solo, there are multiple footwork stylings the Follow can choose from. Four fun possibilities are described below.

If there are multiple six-counts of Follow's Solo, the Follow can keep doing her favorite styling the whole time, try a different styling each time, or even mix and match halves (as in the Feather Stitch styling described on the next page).

Leads, how do you lead which one she does? You don't: it's her choice. If she seems like she's having fun being creative, give her more bars of Follow's Solo (as long as you're not blocking traffic), but once she seems ready for something new, move on to something else.

∞

Touches Styling in Follow's Solo [FST]

(1) A cross-step L.

(2) Touch R to the right side, open, without weight.

(3) Twist CCW to face the opposite direction, keeping R free, lightly touching the floor.

(4-5-6) Repeat opposite.

∞

Sweeps Styling in Follow's Solo [FSS]

(1) A cross-step L.

(2-3) Make a sweeping glissade (*ronde de jambe*) with your R toe, circling from behind, around CCW, toward the front, toe low to the floor. Follow through with your whole body, rotating halfway CCW to face against LOD.

(4-5-6) Repeat opposite, threading the needle with your R foot straight through the space between your left leg and his right leg into the cross-step, then sweeping with your L as you rotate halfway CW to face along LOD.

Flicks Styling in Follow's Solo [FSF]

(1) A cross-step L.

(2) Touch R to the right side, open, without weight, turning to face the opposite direction.

(3) Flick R into the air behind you. For more of a Tango styling, keep the right knee close to the left knee, rather than letting the knees separate.

∞

Feather Stitch Styling in Follow's Solo [FSJ]

This is inspired by a 1913 Tango figure by Joan Sawyer.

(1-2-3) Sweeps Styling, from above.

(4-5-6) Basic step, with three weight changes.

∞

Counter Crossing [CCR]

This is a variation of Follow's Solo in which the Lead also dances, with cross-steps in opposition to the Follow's.

(1-2-3) Follow's Solo. On (3), the Lead shifts back to take weight off his R.

(4-5-6) As he leads his partner into her secondary cross-step, he re-steps on his R, into a non-turning basic. At this moment, the dancers are both crossing R in front in opposite directions, both doing the right-footed half of the basic.

(1-2-3) Both do the left-footed half of the basic. The Lead must clearly lead his partner "past his pocket" in the opposite direction, each time.

To exit:

(1-2-3) Both do the left-footed half of a basic, but the Lead stops with his right foot free, ready to cross into a Turning Basic on the next count (1).

(4-5-6) Keeping his right foot free, he leads the Follow to finish the second half of the basic.

(1) Both begin a Turning Basic with the primary cross-step.

When Counter Crossing, both partners can do any of the stylings that the Follow used in Follow's Solo. You can match your partner's style, or both choose your own.

The next family of variations was inspired by a 1914 Tango figure by Joan Sawyer.

Follow's Solo Corte

This can either be done on the primary cross-step of a repeated Follow's Solo, or it can be started immediately on any primary cross-step.

(1-2-3) First half of Follow's Solo, but bringing the Follow in front of the Lead, facing straight back at him on (2-3).

(4) The Lead invites the Follow to lunge forward toward him with her R as he steps back L.

∞

That's great, but how do you get out of it? It depends how dramatic the lunge is.

Follow's Solo Corte with Outside Turn Exit [FCO]

If the lunge is a dramatic one, hold (4-5-6), use (1-2-3) to replace out of it (Lead forward R, Follow back L), rotating the Follow to face forward along LOD, then lead a single Follow's outside turn along LOD on (4-5-6).

∞

Follow's Solo Corte with Double Outside Turn Exit [FCD]

If the lunge is easier to recover from, you can exit with a double turn.

Hold (4-5-6), then start turning the Follow CW, leading her to step back L on (1) and forward R on (2) into a regular double outside turn on (2-3-4-5-6).

This could also be a **Follow's Solo Corte with Outside Turn and Free Spin Exit**.

∞

Waterfall Follow's Solo [WFS]

This is a Follow's Solo that starts on the second half.

(1-2-3) The first half of Waterfall.

(4-5-6) The Lead steps back L as in Waterfall and stops there on (4) while leading the Follow forward into the second half of a Follow's Solo, with the Follow at the Lead's right side, on the inside lane. She crosses R in front of L along LOD and turns CW to face the hands, which are pointed against LOD.

(1-2-3) The first half of Follow's Solo, with the Follow crossing L against LOD, turning CCW.

(4-5-6) Exit into the second half of Waterfall, starting with the Lead crossing L behind and the Follow crossing R in front.

The Follow can use any Follow's Solo footwork styling in this variation as well.

∞

Tsunami [TSU]

This elegant combination was named by Walter Dill.

Simply do the first two bars of Waterfall Follow's Solo (half Turning Basic and half Solo) twice in a row, returning to place and then continuing on, or repeating it back and forth in place.

If the Follow catches the Solo in time, it's even more fun when she adds Sweeps styling, for a **Tsunami with Sweeps** [TSS].

If you invert the halves, doing a regular Follow's Solo on the first half, and the second half of Waterfall on the second half, it's a **U-Turn** [UTU].

If you do only half of Tsunami (or U-Turn), you'll end up facing the opposite way, which is a useful if you ever find yourself traveling against LOD (into traffic).

∞

Tsunami with Inside Turn [TIN]

This option for varying the second half of Tsunami was invented by UT student Cooper Fryar.

The Lead does both halves of Tsunami, while leading the Follow into the first half of Tsunami, then a cross-body inside turn into the inside lane starting on the second (2).

Her footwork for the second half is: cross (1), back (2), forward (3), back (4), then side against LOD (5), and side along LOD (6).

∞

Molinete [MOL]

(1) Primary cross-step diagonally toward the center of the room.

(2) The Lead rotates the Follow CCW to face him squarely as he rocks forward L toward her, and she rocks back R away from him.

(3) He rocks (replaces) back away from her onto his R, as she rocks (replaces) forward L toward him, both rotating CCW together.

(4-5) Rock two more steps back and forth, continuing to rotate CCW. These almost feel like baby left-turning pivot steps.

(6) Both recover with a step along LOD.

∞

Hesitating Tango Lunge [TLG]

(1-2) Primary cross-step along LOD, with a slight lunge (1), and hold (2).

(3) Replace back onto outside foot.

(4-5) Side step against LOD on the rear foot, facing partner, standing taller (4), and hold (5).

(6) Both replace forward along LOD with outside feet, ready to re-commence with the primary cross-step on (1).

∞

Promenade Media Luna [MED]

(1) A non-rotating cross-step along LOD, planting weight on that foot.

(2-3) Both sweep outside foot out and around to point it in front along LOD without weight. This can be led with both a physical lead of an inward rotation of the frame, as well as a visual lead of the Lead looking down at the sweeping feet and the Follow following his gaze and mirroring him.

(4-5-6) Both sweep outside foot out and around to the back, then pass it straight forward just to the outside of the inside foot into a step forward along LOD on (6).

∞

Media Luna Mendocina [MEN]

This is adapted from a Tango figure in Nicanor Lima's *El Tango Argentino de Salon* from Buenos Aires, c. 1916.

(1-2-3) Three-step grapevine along LOD, Lead crossing behind, stepping side, and crossing in front as the Follow crosses in front, steps side, and crosses behind.

(4-5-6) Side step along LOD (4), holding (5), then replace side against LOD (6).

(1-2-3) Three-step grapevine against LOD, Lead crossing in front, stepping side, and crossing behind as the Follow crosses behind, steps side, and crosses in front.

(4-5-6) Side step against LOD (4), holding (5), then replace side along LOD (6).

Repeat, or the Lead crosses in front with the Follow into a primary cross-step on (1).

This variation majorly blocks traffic, so maybe do it in the center of the room.

∞

Rueda [RDA]

On (1), the Lead crosses R tightly over L with weight and slowly twists CCW on the balls of both feet to unwind his feet while he leads the Follow to walk CCW around him. Then he re-crosses to join her on the next (1) into a Turning Basic. Follows, stay close to the Lead, walking in a perfect circle around him, to avoid pulling him over.

If the Lead just steps in place while leading the Follow around him instead of crossing over and twisting to unwind, it's called **The Eddy** [EDD].

∞

Grapevine Rueda [GRD]

After a Six-Count Grapevine, the Lead crosses R tightly over L and holds, turning CCW to unwind his feet while the Follow grapevines around him for six more steps, starting by crossing L behind on (1). Leads, even though you're stationary, you still need to clearly lead her grapevine. Once again, Follows, stay close to the Lead, to avoid pulling him over.

∞

Waterwheel [WTW]

(1-2-3) First half of Waterfall, keeping the Lead facing against LOD going into (4).

(4-5-6) The Lead keeps the Follow at his right side and walks forward into the center of the room around his partner, while leading the Follow to walk forward around him into the outside lane, rotating CW in place as a couple.

(1-2-3) Continue to walk forward around each other, rotating CW as a couple. The Lead is now going into the outside lane.

(4-5-6) Keep rotating until the Follow is in the outside lane, then rotate her to face forward along LOD on (5-6).

At the end, you'll have completed two full rotations, a half turn every three counts.

Waterwheel Outside Turn [WTO]

If you rotate slightly faster and get the Follow in the outside lane before the final (4-5-6), that last bar can be a Follow's outside turn along LOD.

∞

Scorpion Side Steps [SCO]

(1) A non-rotating cross-step along LOD.

(2) Side step along LOD, staying in your own lane, in Scorpion Position, which means raising curved arms (his left, her right) into a scorpion's tail overhead, looking back against LOD.

(3) Close rear foot to front foot with weight.

(4-5) Repeat (2) and (3).

(6) Side step along LOD, starting to face forward along LOD, and bringing the arms back to regular waltz position.

∞

Scorpion Inside Turn [SCI]

(1-2-3) Half of a Turning Basic.

(4-5-6) Three dramatic steps forward along LOD over the elbows in Scorpion position, this time with the tail pointing and your eyes looking in the direction of travel.

(1-6) The last two bars of He Goes, She Goes. The Scorpion hands come through the frame to lead the Follow's inside turn, then the Lead sweeps the Follow across LOD to the outside lane.

As the second half of this variation is the same as the second half of He Goes, She Goes, anything that modifies or comes out of the second half of He Goes, She Goes can modify or come out of a Scorpion Inside Turn.

∞

The description of one of the best Tango-inspired figures, the **Hesitating Tango Dip**, will be saved until Chapter 27, "Ways to Conclude a Waltz with Flair," which includes many tips for dipping safely.

Chapter 13

Mistakes

Social and competition ballroom dance are both valid pursuits, but they're different from each other in many ways. A big difference is the attitude concerning mistakes.

In competitions, judges deduct points for every mistake, so competition dance culture is aligned against making mistakes from day one. When a dancer misses a step or does something unintended, it's considered a mistake, something to be eliminated. Competitive dancers work hard to achieve 100%.

In social dancing, mistakes are accepted as inevitable. Social dancers laugh them off and move on, happy if things work out 80% of the time. The other 20% is when most learning happens.

Besides, mistakes aren't always mistakes. The Follow made a valid alternate interpretation of the lead, not a mistake. And maybe the Lead accidentally created something that was fun and didn't feel wrong.

That's an important distinction. If you have the common mindset of, "Did I do that right?" you can make an easy shift to, "I enjoyed that, and it didn't feel wrong." That first response feels like it has only one correct answer; the second response has infinite answers.

Think of that first nanosecond of a mistake as the beginning of something new. At that first moment of "Oops!" see if you can welcome that chance intrusion as an opening to a new figure, or a new conclusion to the figure that was intended.

Think of it as exploring new territory. Think of it as making something up as you go. It's creative expression.

Be curious. Learn from mistakes.

What do we want to learn? How to avoid future mistakes? No, that's competition ballroom. We want to learn what else is possible. And we learn how to keep moving through a mistake, as if it were intentional.

> "Intelligence is not to make no mistakes,
> but to see how to make them good."
>
> — Bertolt Brecht

Here is some advice for Follows from Argentine Tango instructor Susana Miller:

> Don't try to be correct. Don't avoid mistakes, or your feet will have tension. Rather, make mistakes freely, and enjoy them. Step wherever you step, boldly and confidently.

And here is some advice for Leads from Stanford student Vince Ranganathan:

> I often apologize. I say "sorry" for the misstep, for mixing up two moves, or for not communicating my intentions better. I say sorry with the hope that my partner doesn't lose faith and rolls with it, and we move on.
>
> There are times when an apology is necessary, like when toes are stepped on. But the reality is that most of the time, an apology isn't necessary. I've realized that it's actually detrimental to repeatedly apologize for small errors. It signals to my partner, "I have no idea what I'm doing, sorry you have to deal with this," and gives them reason to give up as well.
>
> But if instead I laugh it off, then they laugh too. The interaction changes, from me annoying them with redundant apologies, to us sharing smiles. And then it's an upward spiral of energy from there. The message that I convey is "I made a mistake but it's no big deal, let's keep going and have some fun with it!" And the reception is more positive than it is with self-deprecation.
>
> So my plan of action when I screw up is to laugh. At worst, I'll look a little silly, but I'll have good time. At best, my partner will start laughing too, and we'll both have a good time. When the other option is saying sorry twenty times and ending the dance on awkward terms, there's really no decision to be made.

> "The art of being wise is
> the art of knowing what to overlook."
>
> — William James

Chapter 14

Don't Mind the Mess-Ups

Brandon Azad re-took the introductory social dance class at Stanford as a Follow, and wrote this essay about his experience.

∞

I've taken intro social dance before, as a Lead, over a year ago now, and I remember worrying that my partners were not enjoying themselves if I messed something up, or didn't remember all the figures we had learned. And I apologized profusely.

However, taking the class from the Follow's perspective has helped me appreciate that partnering is an unscripted communication, and while sometimes things don't work out as intended, that's not necessarily a bad thing, certainly not something that one should feel bad for. Dancing from the Follow's perspective I would occasionally see the same guilt and apology that I once felt. But on none of those occasions was I not having a blast. I from a year ago probably wouldn't have believed that I as a Follow really do not mind the "mess ups." I definitely wouldn't have believed that half the time I have heard "oops" or "sorry" while following, I didn't even notice any awkwardness in the dance at all.

Realizing that I still enjoy dancing as a Follow when my partner "messes up" has really boosted my confidence as both a Lead and a Follow. Before, I took the phrase "the Lead is dancing for the Follow" too literally: I worried that my indecision or unclear leads would ruin my partner's experience. I now understand that "dancing for your partner" doesn't mean "perfectly, so that she knows exactly where to go and when," but rather…"in dialogue with your partner." The point is to be there for your partner, to keep communication open, as each figure flows into the next, and enjoy each other's company.

"We don't make mistakes.
We do variations."

— Sign hanging in
Campbell Miller's living room

Chapter 15

Musicality in Cross-Step Waltz

Music has often been described as the soul of dance. It drives our dancing, both physically and emotionally. Therefore, ideal dance partnering is often described as a three-way collaboration between the Lead, the Follow, and the music, with each contributing equally to the dance.

Whenever we ask dancers what qualities they admire most in their partners, musicality is always high on the list. Fortunately, musicality isn't some mysterious gift which some people are born with, but rather a few easy awarenesses that can help enhance our dancing. For both roles, musicality primarily arises from truly listening to the music.

Music isn't just a metronome: it has many layers, dynamics, and textures. Therefore, rather than counting the beats, or analytically thinking about the elements of music, feel its emotional content. Lose yourself in the music. Let it carry you along its journey. Embody it with your dancing. As the saying goes, "dancing is music made visible."

That being said, there are some specific pieces of advice we can give you for dancing more musically, which we'll share in the rest of this chapter. But if these suggestions are too much for you to think about while dancing, just focus on truly listening to and feeling the music. That's the most important part. If you do that, the rest will eventually come naturally.

Match the Beats

The most basic starting point for musicality is to step exactly to the beat of the music—not ahead or behind the beat or faster or slower than the tempo. There are both positive and negative motivations for doing this. On one hand, it's a wonderful sensation to feel exactly in sync with a dance partner as you move together to music. On the other hand, it's frustrating for a Follow to be led to dance off the beat, and frustrating for a Lead to figure out how to lead a Follow who is dancing off the beat.

Of course, some songs include a bit of *rubato* (Italian for "stolen time"), which is a slight speeding up or slowing down of the tempo. Even in this case, you'll want to stay right on the music, speeding up or slowing down your dancing to match it perfectly.

It's important to note that Follows are often better at this than Leads. This has nothing to do with gender: it's simply that the Lead role is often preoccupied with thinking about what and how to Lead, while the Follow role is based on listening, literally and figuratively, for signals and embodying them. This means that the Follow often hears the music better than the Lead.

Therefore, Follows can often help their partners stay on time by stepping precisely on the beat themselves, which serves as a sort of physical amplification of the music. This will often help their partners shift from slightly off the beat to right on it. (This also works for helping Follows too, in cases where the Lead happens to be the one who is more on the beat.)

In either role, if you notice that your partner is off the beat, you can either try to guide them onto the beat, or you can test your own leading/following skills by matching their timing, which can actually be a fun challenge. But in general, dancing on the beat is a precondition for more advanced levels of musicality.

Note: This last point is generally true in Cross-Step Waltz, but doesn't necessarily apply to other dances like Tango or Blues (p. 207) that encourage dancers to play around with the timing, as a jazz singer would.

Match the Downbeat

Just as Cross-Step Waltz has two halves, with a primary and a secondary cross-step, the music also has two halves, with a primary downbeat (1), and a secondary downbeat (4). In order to make the dance feel most musical, it's important to align the primary cross-step with the primary downbeat. This means traveling toward the held hands on (1), and toward the rear elbows on (4).

$$\mathbf{1}\,2\,3\,/\,\mathbf{4}\,5\,6$$

Most Cross-Step Waltz songs consistently alternate between (1) and (4) every three counts, which means all you need to do is start at (1), and come back to it after every variation (of 6, 12, or 18 counts), and you'll always be matching the downbeat. But some songs have extra or missing bars. Rather than the usual eight bars to a phrase (more on this in a moment), they have an occasional phrase of 7 (a missing bar), 9 (an extra bar), or some other odd number.

In this case, to match the music, you'll want to find a way to get back on the primary downbeat: the easiest method is to dance Stop and Go (p. 20). As soon as you hear that you're off the downbeat, dance Stop and Go and you'll be back on it. If you know the song and can predict when the extra bar is coming, you can dance Stop and Go on that odd bar, and you'll never be off the music.

Alternatively, as a more advanced option, you could transition to Role Reversal (p. 171) or Mirror Waltz (p. 185), which would put the new primary cross-step on the new primary downbeat without having to use Stop and Go as you usually would. Or you could transition to another dance (p. 199), which also usually shifts the downbeat.

Occasionally, a song will have extra or missing beats. In this case, you'll end up dancing on the 2, 3, 5, or 6. An elegant way to fix this is to dance one or two four-count Single Pivots (p.

104) to shift you back onto the 1 or 4. Another option is simply to dance Waltz Walk (p. 19) for a few counts until you can cross into a Turning Basic on 1 or 4. (If you're dancing on the 2, 4, or 6, you won't be able to get back to the 1 without changing your feet with something like Stop and Go.) Alternatively, you could simply dance Stop and Go with an extended pause to fix any kind of downbeat problem you might be facing. But however you do it, your partner will appreciate getting back to the downbeat.

Match the Phrasing

Dancing is more satisfying when the phrasing of the dance matches the phrasing of the music. Music has punctuation marks, so to speak: commas, semicolons, periods, exclamation marks, etc. Dance has similar punctuation marks. Punctuate the music with your dancing.

As we noted in the previous section, most Cross-Step Waltz music has eight bars to a phrase. This means that as we listen to the song, there's a clear sense that something is coming to an end on the eighth bar and something new is beginning on the first bar of the next phrase.

1 2 3 / **2** 5 6 / **3** 2 3 / **4** 5 6 / **5** 2 3 / **6** 5 6 / **7** 2 3 / **8** 5 6 /

There are two main ways you can approach matching the phrasing. The first approach, which is slightly easier, is to line up the beginning of a variation with the beginning of the phrase, i.e., to wait until the major downbeat to start something new. For example, start He Goes, She Goes on bar 1, concluding it on bar 4, and then finish out the phrase with four bars (two full turns) of Turning Basic.

The second approach, which is slightly more challenging but often even more satisfying, is to line up the end of the variation with the end of the phrase. For example, if you want to dance He Goes, She Goes, a four-bar figure, dance four bars (two full turns) of Turning Basic first, then finish out the phrase with the figure. The Follow's sweep across into waltz position at the end will be particularly satisfying when it lines up perfectly with the end of the phrase.

Of course, these approaches aren't mutually exclusive. They're quite complementary. The goal is simply to line up beginnings with beginnings and endings with endings. Start things at the beginning of the phrase, and wrap things up at the end of the phrase, and you'll be well on your way to better musicality.

As you might imagine, it's easy to go a bit overboard on this. If a Lead is solely focused on the goal of matching up beginnings and endings, he's going to be paying so much attention to the music that he won't be paying as much attention to his partner. Therefore, rather than trying to hit every beginning and ending, just try to hit some of them.

In particular, you'll notice that some phrase changes make a bigger impact than others. In addition to the phrase change every eight bars, there are also larger changes within a song, often at 16 or 32 bars. These mark a transition between different movements of a song, for example, the verse and chorus. Because these larger shifts are particularly noticeable, they're a great place to start experimenting with phrase-based musicality.

Matching the phrasing will often require a few seconds of delayed gratification for the Lead. Your inclination might be to lead a variation the moment it pops into your head. To you, that would be spontaneous, intuitive dancing. But the Follow isn't reading your mind. The Follow is dancing to the music. So when the idea of a variation occurs to you, hold that thought for a few seconds so that you can lead it when it will be most musical. While the Follow will probably enjoy the variation in any case, this way will leave her thinking, "Wow, everything's so musical with *him!*" You want to be that *him*.

Similarly, when transitioning from one dance to another (p. 199), time the transition to occur when the music changes, where the Follow will most likely expect a change. She'll appreciate it happening where she expected it, as if you were reading her mind.

On that note, Follows, while you want to be paying attention at all times, be particularly attentive at musical moments, such as phrase changes. Just as Follows find it particularly satisfying when a Lead leads a variation at a musical moment, Leads find it particularly satisfying when Follows are also fully engaged in those moments, allowing the variations to happen so naturally that it feels like the decision to dance that particular variation was mutual.

A potential danger of this piece of advice for Follows is that expecting something to happen at musical moments can become one more way for us to unnecessarily disapprove of our partners, and another way to disappoint ourselves. Another potential danger is that you might interpret this advice to mean that you can pay less attention in the middle of a musical phrase, but of course that's not what we're suggesting. Instead, be ready all the time, and especially ready in these musical moments. Then enjoy whatever variation comes next, even if you were expecting it to be something else.

At this point, it's important to pause and note once again that for all of the different kinds of musicality we've looked at so far—matching the beat, the downbeat, and the phrase—the ideal is not to be constantly counting and calculating. You may need to do that in the beginning, but in the end, this approach is far too formulaic. Ultimately, musicality is more art than science.

Just relax and listen closely to the music, intuitively sensing where the beat, downbeat, and phrase changes are. The more music you listen and dance to, the more you will internalize its structure and know when something is coming, rather than having to count everything.

Match the Quality

Even when they share the same beat structure, tempo, and phrasing, different songs feel completely different. Listening through a playlist of Cross-Step Waltz music, many different adjectives come to mind—bluesy, cheerful, dreamy, driving, epic, haunting, hopeful, longing, mysterious, reverent, somber, triumphant—to name just a few.

Whatever qualities you hear in the music, try to embody those same qualities in your dancing. For Leads, these qualities can certainly influence your choice of variations. But even more importantly, for both Leads and Follows, these qualities can—and should—influence *how* you dance each variation.

The idea here is that even if you danced the exact same variations to two different songs, the two dances would look and feel different, sometimes dramatically so. For example, the way you dance to "Arwen's Vigil" by The Piano Guys should be different from the way you dance to "The Hard Way" by Fort Minor, which should be different from the way you dance to "Is This Love" by Corinne Bailey Rae.

It's important to note that there's no one right or wrong way to do this. How you choose to interpret the various musical qualities of each song is up to you. But it's something you want to be aware of, letting the qualities of the music naturally influence your movements. The point is not to anlayze, "the music is bluesy, so that means I need to move my arms this way." The point is to deeply listen to the music and let it move you, both figuratively and literally.

Often, Follows are better at this aspect of musicality than Leads (sometimes *much* better), for the same reason we discussed above. Therefore, in many dance forms, including Cross-Step Waltz, it's often the Follow who initiates the styling of the dance, while the Lead initiates the patterns. Just as the Follow follows the patterns initiated by the Lead, the Lead can follow the styling initiated by the Follow. Of course, this isn't a hard and fast rule: Leads can also influence the styling, just as Follows can influence the patterns. But in general, it's a convenient division of labor. Not that any of this is actually labor! (For more on that, see "Work and Play" on p. 205.)

Match the Energy

One specific quality of the music that's worth singling out is its energy. Some Cross-Step Waltz music provides a lot of energy, while other songs are more subdued. In addition, each song has its own internal highs and lows.

As a Lead, you want to make sure that the variations you're leading are supported by the music, i.e., save high-energy variations for high-energy music, and relax with easygoing variations when the music is relaxed.

As a Follow, you'll want to interpret each variation with the appropriate energy as well: when the musical energy is high, yours should be too, and vice versa.

Match the Moments

In addition to the basic elements of beats, phrasing, quality, and energy, many songs include specific moments that ask for something different. For example, in Sheryl Crow's "Stop," the music dramatically cuts out for six counts at multiple points in the song. These moments demand something different from your dancing.

In this particular example, there are two different approaches you could take: 1) you could listen to Sheryl Crow and literally do something that stops, e.g., a Hesitating Side Sway (p. 20), or 2) you could do something dramatic and dynamic to fill the space that's been created, e.g., Double Pivots (p. 106). Both options are equally satisfying in different ways.

Other moments are more subtle. Some songs have moments that sound like pivots, or a grapevine, or a flurry of turns. See how closely you can match your dancing to the music by choosing variations and stylings that are the physical embodiment of what you hear in the music. Other songs have different beats emphasized. While (1) is still the downbeat, maybe (2) is emphasized, or (3). See if you can make things happen on these counts, e.g., a turn that's led on (2), or one that's prepped on (3).

Follows, you can also use these musical moments to guide your dancing, whether it's in terms of your footwork, styling, or how quickly you turn.

Match the Lyrics

In some dances, like West Coast Swing, the lyrics of a song also have a major influence on the dance. In these dances, one of the goals of more experienced dancers is to line up the content of the dance with the content of the song. Of course, you don't want to do this formulaically, miming every word of the song. But some of the most satisfying moments in West Coast Swing are those in which the words of the singer are brought to life on the dance floor.

While this isn't always possible in Cross-Step Waltz (a dance which often has instrumental music), it can be fun to try this occasionally, when it happens to work out. We already saw one example of this: stopping when Sheryl Crow says "stop." Other Cross-Step Waltz songs include lyrics like "holding hands," "round and round," "hold without touching," "don't let go," and "feel our bodies sway." These are just some of the most obvious lyrical moments you might play with: others can be a bit more figurative.

This is higher-level musicality, as it requires knowing the song, anticipating the moment, and working together to hit it perfectly. No one is expecting you to do this. But if you've mastered all of the other forms of musicality, and you're dancing to a favorite song with a favorite partner, it's an amazing feeling when you can hit these kinds of moments.

Match Your Partner

While musicality can be a lot of fun, it can also be a distraction from the real goal of dancing: meaningfully connecting with your partner.

As Follows, we've all danced with that one Lead who's doing his own thing to the music, with no regard for the fact that you have your own feelings. It's no fun to feel like a puppet. Similarly, as Leads, we've all danced with that one Follow who's doing her own thing to the music, with no regard for you either.

In social dancing, your partner is primary. In either role, go along with what your partner is doing, rather than making them a slave to your interpretation of the music. As a Lead, always track and adapt to your partner, even if that means missing a musical moment. As a Follow, listen to your partner before the music, even if he misses a musical moment.

While we've discussed many different kinds of musicality in this chapter, it's important for dancers of both roles not to view these as new ways to judge your partner. Freestyle social dancing is challenging enough as it is, even without considering musicality. Therefore, accept your partner for who they are, regardless of how musical they may be.

As a specific tip, count each awesome musical moment as a win, and don't even think about the "losses." Depending on who you're dancing with, the wins might be as large as perfectly hitting every musical moment in the whole song, or as small as occasionally getting the cross-step on the downbeat. Regardless of their size, these are all wins nonetheless!

In either role, if you want to help your partner become more musical, be especially encouraging of their musical successes, either verbally ("that was awesome!") or simply by offering an even bigger smile than usual. When your partner sees how much you enjoy those moments, they'll want to become even more musical in the future.

Developing Musicality

As with all of the other aspects of dancing, developing musicality takes time, and follows the trajectory described in the "Conscious Competence" chapter of our first book, *Waltzing*.

First, you won't even be aware of musicality (Unconscious Incompetence). Then you'll be aware of it, but know you're not very good at it (Conscious Incompetence). As you get better at dancing Cross-Step Waltz, you'll slowly begin to dance more musically by devoting more conscious attention to the music, perhaps even counting the beats and phrases in your head (Conscious Competence). Eventually, when you spend enough time listening and dancing, musicality will simply become a part of your dancing without having to count it out or think about it, and you'll naturally adapt to the music, even when the song is one you haven't heard before (Unconscious Competence).

As a specific tip to improve your musicality in Cross-Step Waltz, listen to more Cross-Step Waltz music (p. 221), even—perhaps especially—when you're not dancing. While you're dancing, the music is only one of your many focuses, which means that when you're not dancing, you can pay even greater attention to it. Play it in the car as you're driving to work, or in the kitchen while you're doing the dishes. Maybe even listen to it as you're falling asleep. The more you surround yourself with Cross-Step Waltz music in your everyday life, the better you will get at interpreting it on the dance floor.

We can always get better at dancing musically, just as we can always get better at dancing for our partners. Put these two pursuits together, and you will gain the enhanced pleasure of a truly musical conversation between yourself, your partner, and the music, moving together in perfect three-part harmony.

"Music gives
a soul to the universe,
wings to the mind,
flight to the imagination,
a charm to sadness,
and life to everything."

— Plato

Chapter 16

Conversations

An essay by Stanford student Eleanor Collier.

∞

This past quarter, I've had some incredible conversations. Very few of them have involved any talking. Instead, I have learned to converse through movement, through the subtle voice of two bodies connecting.

Part of the joy of this conversation is speaking. This quarter I stopped trying to dance the "right way" or execute figures with perfect precision, and started moving my body in a way that expresses who I am, that shouts my intrinsic joy for living. As my voice in dance has grown in clarity and confidence, so have my interactions outside of dance. I have learned to own the parts of myself that are silly, flawed, and idiosyncratic, and to say them as loudly (or quietly) as they need to be said.

Equally as enjoyable as speaking, if not more enjoyable, is listening. I often close my eyes when I dance—not on purpose, but simply because I get lost in the beautiful silent sound of my partner's voice. Every partner has something different to say. Careful listening makes the difference between speaking and speaking with someone; when partners listen closely to one another, they transform from two people expressing themselves in a self-focused, disconnected manner, into two people communicating, combining their self-expressions in a more beautiful creation than either could create alone.

A third element of the conversation, unique to dance, is the dialogue between both partners and the music. I have realized that music is so much more than a beat to keep track of what step one should be on. It is a tug and pull of sounds and emotions that one can listen and respond to just like another person. The most exquisite moments take place when partners communicate with the music as well as each other.

In short, what I have learned this quarter: Listen, respond. Listen, respond. Listen.

"Dancing's just a conversation
between two people.
Talk to me."

— Justin Matisse in *Hope Floats*

Chapter 17

The French Valse Boston

The French version of Cross-Step Waltz seems to have evolved from Blues steps that Americans brought to Paris in the 1920s.

An article in a 1919 issue of *Dancing Times* magazine correctly reported that Blues is not a dance step, but rather a collection of steps, depending on the music.

In observing the Blues steps that Americans brought over, Parisian dance masters organized these variations into two families of steps: Le Blues and Fox-Blues, which were essentially the One Step and Foxtrot. If the music was walking tempo, dancers did One Step variations (Le Blues), and if the music was quicker, they danced the latest "Jazz" Foxtrot, formerly known as the Two-Step, which was a three-step pattern danced in quick-quick-slow timing (Fox-Blues). In either case, the French liked to begin with the Lead's R, Follow's L.

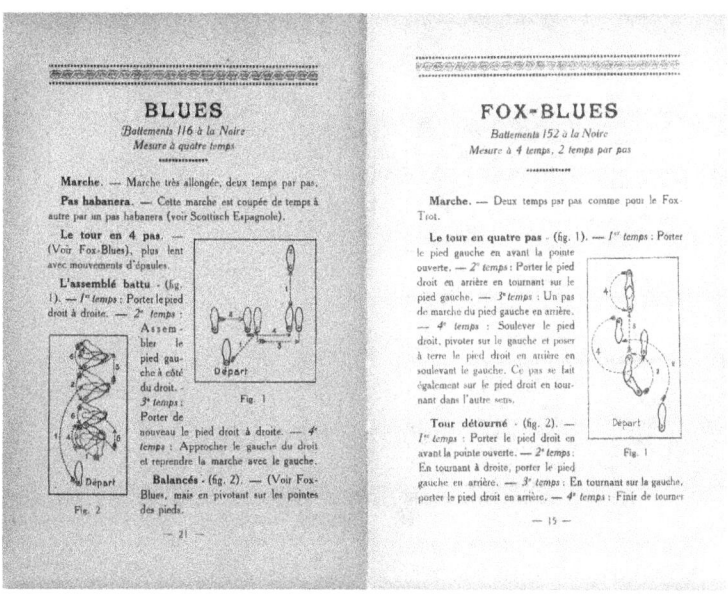

Several French authors of dance manuals in the 1920s described each American dance and variation in detail. Through these dance manuals, we can see the Fox-Blues evolve through that decade, year-by-year.

∞

Pas du Jazz (Straight Jazz) [JPJ]

In closed position, the Lead walks forward along LOD, R-L-R, as the Follow backs up along LOD, L-R-L, in quick-quick-slow timing. Repeat with the opposite foot.

∞

Marche du Côté (Balancé, Pas du Jazz) [JMC]

A sideways Pas du Jazz. The Lead steps side R, close L to R, side R, in quick-quick-slow timing, as the Follow dances the same, L-R-L. Repeat opposite.

∞

Papillon (Balancé, Pas du Jazz) [JPL]

A Marche de Côté danced diagonally, zig-zagging, with the Follow backing up along LOD.

Pas Tournant (Le Jazz en Tournant) [JPT]

The same, rotating, usually CW, although a CCW rotation was sometimes done. In Blues, the rotation need not be a full 360° rotation in two bars, but only rotating only as much as desired.

∞

La Pas Marqué (Pas de Habanera, Le Pas à Point d'Appui) [JPM]

A rocking step in quick-quick-slow timing. Take the first diagonal side step of the Papillon, stopping; rock (replace) back to place; re-take that diagonal step; and rotate a quarter turn, into the other diagonal, on the pause. Repeat toward the other diagonal with opposite feet.

∞

Pas Titubé ("Staggering Step") [JTB]

This is the Blues step that likely evolved into the French Cross-Step Waltz.

Take the first diagonal side step of the Papillon; the Lead crosses the next step behind as the Follow crosses over in front; then take another diagonal side step. Quick-quick-slow. Repeat toward the other diagonal with opposite feet, the Lead again crossing behind as the Follow crosses in front, on the second step.

∞

Pas Croisés [JPC]

Five years later, the Pas Titubé was described with both dancers crossing in front on the second step, while rotating a little, CW.

∞

Jazz Roll [JJR]

This is the Pas Croisés beginning with the cross-step. The Lead crosses R in front as the Follow crosses L in front; both step side; both replace, pulling that foot back a little. The timing is now changed to slow-quick-quick. This was also done rotating.

∞

French Valse Boston [FVB]

This is the Jazz Roll danced to slow waltz music, in even timing (all quick steps). This step evolved around 1930, when slow waltz music became popular.

Paris in the Jazz Age

The dances of 1920s Paris are fascinating to study on their own merits, but their appeal is greatly enhanced by their setting in one of the brightest cultural flowerings of the century.

Dancing in Paris ceased during World War I, but within weeks of the Armistice, Parisians were dancing again "with their traditional *furia francese*." Even though public dancing was still prohibited at the end of 1918, many balls were given by the various regiments, with even more "private" tea dances held by the numerous dance teachers. In 1919, dancing in Paris fully returned to its pre-war frenzy. "The world is dance mad," wrote a Monsieur Pierre, "but the visitor in Paris will soon come to the conclusion that the craze has reached its paroxysm in the French capital." *The Dancing Times* reported that, "They apparently cannot take a meal or watch a play through without breaking off for a round or two of dancing."

As with the pre-war dance craze, the renewed love of dancing included a fondness for variety. The One Step, Hesitation Waltz, and Boston remained essentially unchanged, but the Foxtrot and Argentine Tango evolved forward to a significant extent. La Java, a rustic mazurka from the Parisian outskirts, enjoyed a new popularity. Shimmy and Toddle, which were jazzy styles of bouncing the Foxtrot, were borrowed from the Americans. The Paso Doble and Scottisch Espagnole were imported from Spain, the Milonga from Argentina, and the Samba from Brazil. The U.S. continued to be a principal source for choreographic innovations, with Le Blues becoming a new favorite, followed by the Charleston and Black Bottom. Dancing in Paris saw a variety unmatched in England, Germany, or the United States.

Parisians didn't need to travel to the U.S. to pick up the latest dance steps; thousands of Americans brought them to Paris. War veterans stayed on after wartime duty in France. Pleasure-seekers fled the restrictions of the American prohibition era. And tourists were attracted to the post-war economy which made the dollar tremendously valuable in France. When the dollar reached a record high of fifty francs in the mid-twenties, a dollar bought a month's supply of bread in Paris, and one could obtain passage across the Atlantic for $80.

Back then, the American presence was welcome—and fashionable. The French called their tea *dansants* "Dancings," just as French terms were used for New York clubs. Dance music was provided by touring American bands or by French approximations of the jazz sound. Parisian establishments also welcomed the visitors' money, and the government levied an entrance tax of 25 to 33 percent on all Dancings and restaurants which included dance orchestras.

The most influential artists of the earlier Belle Epoch had shunned the high life of society, but the literary, artistic, and musical circles of 1920s Paris often partied along with *bon vivants* from America, England, Spain, and Russia, gathering at the salons of Gertrude Stein and others. The names of those who contributed to the rich artistic and social life of Paris are well-known today. If you were in Paris during the twenties, you could have seen Pablo Picasso, Jean Cocteau, Henri Matisse, Marcel Duchamp, Marc Chagall, Salvador Dali, James Joyce, T. S. Elliot, Ezra Pound, Ernest Hemingway, E. E. Cummings, Gertrude Stein & Alice B. Toklas, F. Scott & Zelda Fitzgerald, Serge Prokofiev, Igor Stravinsky, Erik Satie, Colette, Coco Chanel, Paul Poiret, Josephine Baker, Serge Diaghilev, and Nijinsky.

"The greatest gift we can give one another
is rapt attention to one another's existence."

— Sue Atchley Ebaugh

Chapter 18

Dancing Through Differences

An essay by Stanford student Vanessa Ochavillo.

∞

As a former competitive ballroom dancer, I was conditioned for precision. Every move had a predetermined count, and arms and legs were calculated to the exact degree. When people asked me if I dance, I said yes, but had to clarify that I did choreography, not just dancing. Since taking social dancing, I realized that my categorization as a choreographed dancer was a necessary distinction to make, because never in my career as a trained dancer did I need to think of anyone outside of my self. Sure, I thought about others, but only to match movements to look the same. In contrast, when I would take my partner's hand in social dance, the dance was as much about him as it was about me.

It took longer to internalize this importance difference than I had thought. But maybe about seven weeks into the class, it just clicked. I relaxed the strictness which I had normally applied to footwork and hand placement, and let go of the notion that there was only one correct step. The right step was whatever came out of the combination of my partner's leading and my interpreting. This new mode of thinking made me more easy-going on the dance floor, and I was much happier and better for it.

This newfound acceptance, of whatever the Lead threw out at me, not only made me a better interpreter, but allowed me to better appreciate the different right ways one could do the Waltz, Salsa, Swing, and every other style we danced. In class, as I rotated through different partners every three minutes or so, I would no longer think, "That was weird," I would think, "That was different, but it works." The diversity of people's individual styles is one of the wonders of social dance.

For the first time, I learned what it meant to dance. It was not so much about the precision of performance. Instead, it was about being with people who in that moment participated in the same act, joined by the music. It was about sharing a moment with others—and how in spite of our differences, we were still in step with each other.

"While I dance I cannot judge, I cannot hate,
I cannot separate myself from life.
I can only be joyful and whole.
That is why I dance."

— Hans Bos

Chapter 19

Zig-Zag Variations

As we saw in Chapter 17, Cross-Step Waltz likely evolved from the Pas Titubé, a zig-zagging Foxtrot step that backed the Follow along LOD.

The contemporary Cross-Step Waltz variations in this chapter are based on such a zig-zag.

∞

Zig-Zag [ZIG]

A non-turning basic in which the Lead backs the Follow slowly along LOD. The Lead faces forward along LOD throughout, with the primary cross-step aimed diagonally along LOD into the center, and the secondary cross-step aimed diagonally along LOD toward the outside. The Follow "over-crosses" along the same diagonals, pulling her right shoulder back on the first half, and her left shoulder back on the second half, in order to comfortably cross over in front along the diagonals, as she backs up along LOD.

Leads: Despite the fact that she's backing, carefully lead your partner forward into each cross-step by helping her rotate into each one, rather than just pushing her backward. To see why, try to cross one foot in front of the other as you imagine someone is pushing you backward. It doesn't work for you, so it won't work for her either.

Follows: See if you can outrace your partner along LOD. While you don't *actually* want to outrace him, dancing with this intention which will allow you both to travel more.

∞

Toss Across [TOS]

Same as the Zig-Zag, but sending the Follow across from one half-closed position (Lead's right arm under Follow's left) to the other (Lead's left arm under Follow's right).

Zig-Zag with Lead Crossing Behind [ZLB]

This is a phase-shifted, waltz-time version of the 1920s Pas Titubé (p. 81) that likely evolved into the French cross-step Valse Boston.

It's simply a Zig-Zag in which the Lead crosses behind on (1) and (4), instead of in front. The Lead still faces forward along LOD, or more specifically, diagonally forward to the outside wall on (1), and diagonally forward to the center on (4).

∞

Follow's Backing Ochos [ZFB]

This is actually an old slow waltz variation that predated the popularity of Cross-Step Waltz.

It's a Zig-Zag in which the Follow crosses behind on (1) and (4), instead of in front, as the Lead crosses in front each time.

To get into it, the Lead catches the Follow on (5-6) of a Turning Basic, keeping her back facing diagonally along LOD into the center of the room, to be oriented to cross back along that diagonal on (1).

To get out of it, keep the Follow in the outside lane on any (5-6), ready to lead into the primary cross-step on (1).

∞

Swingout [SWO]

(1-2-3) The Lead sends the Follow out to swingout position on (1), gently sweeping her past him with his right arm, immediately releasing that arm, keeping her right hand in his left. The Follow dances the first half of a non-turning basic.

(4-5-6) The Lead sweeps the Follow back into closed position by drawing his left hand back toward him. The Follow dances the second half of a non-turning basic into his arms.

This can either be easygoing or dramatic. In the easygoing version, the Lead remains reassuringly close to the Follow as they separate. In the dramatic version, the Lead hangs back away from her.

Hint: For this and all variations based on it, prepare by tucking the hands into swingout handhold, with the Lead's left hand horizontal, and the Follow's right hand hooked over it vertically, instead of being palm to palm, as usual. If you stay palm to palm, the wrists will be uncomfortably bent back in swingout position.

Traveling Swingout [TSO]

This morphs together the Zig-Zag and the Swingout. The Lead sends the Follow toward the center of the room with a cross-body lead on the Zig, connected only by swingout hands, and both return to closed waltz position on the Zag.

∞

Swingout Tuck Turn [STT]

(1-2) Begin a Swingout, but keep the Follow on the outside lane, as the Lead travels forward in the inside lane beside her.

(3) The Lead braces his left hand into the Follow's right hand—hence the "tuck."

Follows: Your footwork on (1-2-3) may naturally turn into a Three-Count Grapevine (p. 44).

(4-5-6) A Follow's outside turn with her footwork pivoting forward, back, foward along LOD.

This could also be a **Swingout Tuck Free Spin** [STF].

∞

Hand-to-Hand Zig-Zag [HZZ]

Do half of a Traveling Swingout on (1-2-3) to get to swingout position. Then sweep the Follow across LOD to the outside lane on (4-5-6) to take right-to-left hands.

Then dance Zig-Zag, holding right-to-left hands for the Zig and change to holding left-to-right hands for the Zag.

∞

Parallel Breaks [PAR]

(1-2-3) The first half of Waterfall.

(4-5-6) As the Lead crosses L behind and the Follow crosses R in front (4), the Lead blocks the Follow and leads her to rock back L as he rocks forward R (5), then both step side toward the outside wall (6). On (4), the partners are right hip to right hip.

(1-2-3) Repeat the previous three counts to the other side, i.e., the Lead crosses R behind as the Follow crosses L in front (1), he rocks forward L as she rocks back right (2), and both step side toward the center of the room (3). On (1), the partners are left hip to left hip.

(4-5-6) Recommence turning with the second half of Waterfall.

Or you can repeat the six-count parallel break, if desired.

"Dancing is the most moving,
the most beautiful of the arts,
because it is no mere translation
or abstraction from life;
it is life itself."

— Havelock Ellis

Chapter 20

How Following Works (and How Leading Can)

Several years ago, Richard and Nick gave Melissa an assignment: to figure out how she follows so well. After several years of thoughtful pondering, here's what she has to report.

The Follow Space

Imagine the set of all possible social dance variations a Follow can be led into: we'll call this the Follow Space.

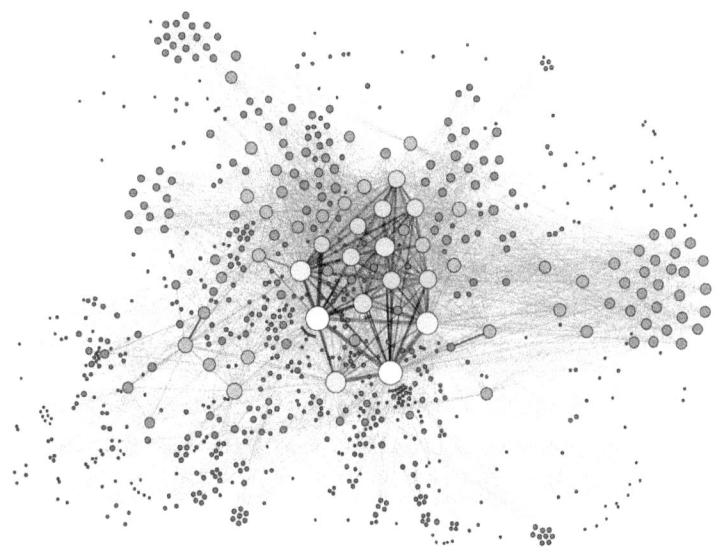

Zooming in, we see that the Follow Space is divided into different worlds that represent each dance style, which are in turn divided into smaller lands that represent different families of variations within those dances, until you get down to individual variations and different stylistic interpretations thereof.

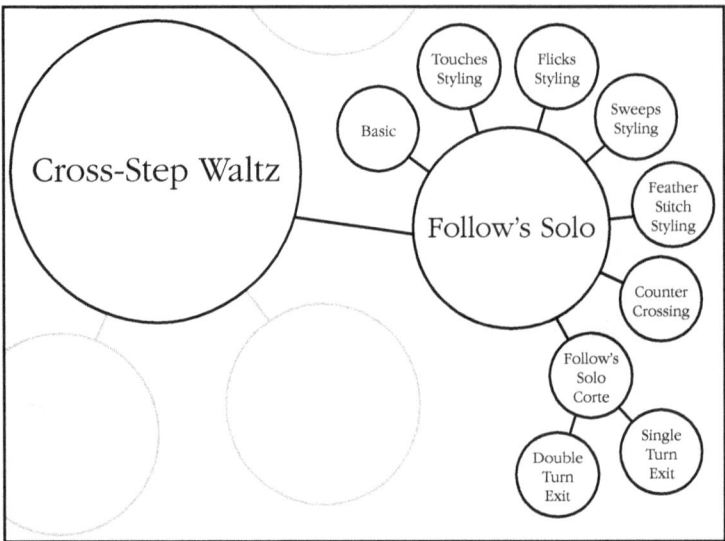

In freestyle social dancing, each time you dance, you'll take a different journey through this space, visiting a different sequence of variations.

In navigating this space, the Follow is in a constant state of discovery, finding new opportunities at every turn. You never know exactly what's going to happen next, but this doesn't mean you have no clue.

Even before the Lead does anything, there are several major constraints to the Follow Space. For example:

- **The Community**: Although the social dance communities at Stanford and UT Austin are quite similar, there are also differences in the vocabulary common to each place. Therefore, depending on whether she's at Stanford's Viennese Ball or UT's Social Dance Soirée, Melissa can expect to be led into different things.

- **The Music**: What kind of music is playing will have a huge influence on which part of the Follow Space you're playing in, i.e., when Cross-Step Waltz music is on, you'll most likely be led into Cross-Step Waltz variations. And even within a given dance style, the unique qualities of each individual song will have a strong influence on what is more or less likely to be led.

- **Experience Level**: If Melissa is dancing with a beginner in her class, where she's taught them everything they know, she can probably expect them to lead some form of the variations she's taught them. But if she's dancing with a more advanced dancer, the Follow Space will have more possibilities.

- **The Lead**: As Melissa dances with each Lead, she will begin to learn what this Lead's vocabulary is, i.e., which parts of the Follow Space he most likes to play in. For example, the figures Richard is most likely to lead may be different from the figures Nick is most likely to lead.

These initial constraints on the Follow Space determine the Follow's initial field of view. As each variation evolves in time, the Follow Space collapses, with the Follow's field of view zooming in on the most likely possibilities.

For example, say Nick and Melissa are dancing Cross-Step Waltz.

It's just before (1). Even before her first step, Melissa is picking up on subtle signals about what's coming next. For example, if Nick is facing forward along LOD and starting to raise his hand, he's probably going to lead into He Goes. If he's facing her and starting to get ahead of her, it's probably going to be something that rotates: a Turning Basic or maybe Pivots. If he's pulling his right shoulder back, it's probably going to be a Grapevine.

In this particular moment, Nick is pulling his right shoulder back as if he's going to cross behind, while leading Melissa's left shoulder forward. At this point, even though she still hasn't taken a single step, Melissa can be 95% confident that what comes next will be based on a Grapevine. This doesn't mean she throws herself into a particular Grapevine variation (or even a Grapevine itself), but it does mean she begins to focus in on the "Grapevines in Cross-Step Waltz" part of the Follow Space and look for further signals that will help her differentiate which kind of Grapevine variation it will be.

For example, going into (3) of the Grapevine, Melissa is particularly sensitive to signals that will help her determine whether it's a Three-Count Grapevine, or a longer one. Are the held hands tucking (or slightly beginning to rise)? Is the parallel-shoulders lead for a Grapevine continuing? Or is something else happening, as in the Pivoting Five-Count Grapevine (p. 49)?

In this case, the parallel-shoulders lead is continuing, so she keeps following that through more steps of a Grapevine, knowing that they're now entering Long Grapevine territory. Therefore, going into (6), she's particularly sensitive to signals that will help her determine whether it's going to be an inside turn on (6), a tuck on (1) into a turn on (2), or something else.

This process of progressively honing in on what the variation will be continues, moment by moment, until the variation is complete, and the process begins again.

It's important to note that in social dancing, the Follow Space never collapses completely: there is never only one correct response to a given signal. Yes, you read that correctly. In fact, you may even want to go back and read it again!

In every variation of every dance, the Follow has options, whether they are footwork substitutions, arm stylings, or even different versions entirely (e.g., a single or multiple free spin). As we'll see later, which of these options the Follow chooses can influence what the Lead does next. But more on that in a bit. First, let's dive a little deeper into how Follows so deftly navigate their ever-evolving journey through the Follow Space.

Following as Autocomplete

Another way of visualizing the Follow's journey through the Follow Space is to think of it as a physical form of autocomplete. As users of any modern device know, autocomplete is a technology that uses the beginning of a word or phrase that has been typed to predict what the end of the word or phrase will be.

For example, if you're writing about food and you start typing "sal," perhaps you're intending to write "salad," "salmon," "salsa," or "salt." An autocomplete algorithm recognizes this, and returns predictions about what the rest of the word will be:

> salad
> salmon
> salsa
> salt

An experienced Follow's brain works in a similar way. As each step is led, it becomes clearer and clearer what the Lead is intending. In our linguistic analogy, once "sal" has been led, the Follow will be particularly sensitive to signals that differentiate whether the next letter will be an "a," "m," "s," or "t." In the real world, after the Lead ducks under into He Goes, the Follow is looking to find out what kind of He Goes variation it will be.

Important Note: While sometimes conscious, this process is often unconscious, so you may not know you're doing it. But even when you're not aware that it's happening, your body is still very much doing this.

Predicting vs. Guessing

This is different from many beginning Follows' tendency to choose one of the options and power themselves through it despite any additional input from the Lead: for example, to throw themselves into "salad" before the second "a" has been led. In physical terms, this would be equivalent to grabbing his hand and powering herself through an inside turn in He Goes, She Goes rather than waiting to see whether it might be a free spin or rollaway.

Instead, an experienced Follow waits to see what the next input is and recalibrates their prediction about what comes next from there. For example, once "sala" has been led, they become particularly sensitive to signals that differentiate "salad" from "salami." For example, going into She Goes, is the hand high or low?

At the same time, an experienced Follow understands that they may also be led into things that they aren't anticipating: the rare case where "sals" turns into "salsify" instead of the more common "salsa." In addition, they understand that they may also be led into variations they've never seen before: the case where "sal" unexpectedly becomes "salisbury steak." So even after they're pretty sure what it will be, they're still open to other possibilities, like He Goes, Double Outside Turn or He Goes, She Goes, She Goes, She Goes.

Ready for Anything?

It's important to note, however, that this openness to possibilities is different from being "ready for anything" at all times, as many teachers (including us) have advised Follows to be. While the best Follows are always open to new possibilities, they are also continuously prepared for potential next steps in direct proportion to their actual likelihood of being led.

In the broadest sense, once it's clear we're dancing Cross-Step Waltz, the Follow will be primarily looking to complete Cross-Step Waltz variations, and will be particularly sensitive to specific signals that differentiate the various steps of Cross-Step Waltz, which will be somewhat different from the signals that differentiate the steps in other dances. In other words, when Cross-Step Waltz music is playing, a Grapevine is infinitely more likely to be led than Charleston Kicks, so the Follow is more prepared for the former than the latter.

On a smaller scale, autocomplete algorithms also use the words that came directly before to make better predictions, for example, "trout and salmon" or "pepper and salt." Similarly, in dancing, the Follow will be particularly ready to dance common combinations of steps, rather than simply following one step at a time. Again, this is different from throwing herself into "trout and salmon," as it may very well be "trout and salad." But by being ready for "salmon," while leaving open the possibility that it might be "salad" (or even "salsify"), she increases her (and her partner's) chance of success. In other words, after a Six-Count Grapevine, the Follow is particularly ready for a Double Turn, while still leaving open the possibility that it might be something else, like a Double Pivot, which is also possible, but far less common.

Just Following?

Of course, some Follows might say, "oh, I'm not really doing any of that, I'm just following." But as we noted before, even if you don't think you're doing this, your body very much is. The fact that it does so is what makes freestyle dancing possible! While some variations in some dances can be led step by step, most variations are actually not. Rather than leading individual steps, Leads signal pieces of variations that are autocompleted by the Follow. For example, in a turn or free spin, he doesn't lead each of her steps one by one: he suggests (and supports) the turn, and she autocompletes it with her preferred footwork (p. 25). If the Follow's body wasn't autocompleting the steps, freestyle dancing would be much more difficult—and in some cases, even impossible.

Viewing following as a form of autocomplete explains where the "mind-reading" quality of the best partnerships come from: it literally is a form of mind-reading, in which she knows (or at least has a very good prediction about) what will come next before he leads it.

Machine Learning

Of course, the autocomplete process will be somewhat different depending on who a Follow is dancing with. While Nick and Richard lead similarly (which makes sense, given that Richard taught Nick), there are also slight differences in the way they lead. Over time, Melissa has learned those differences and adapts her following based on who she's dancing with at the moment. The reason she's particularly good at dancing with them (as compared to another random Lead) is because her algorithms for dancing with them have spent a long time training on each of their datasets, learning what they are each likely to lead and how they are likely to lead it.

By extension, the reason she's so good at following in general is that she has spent a long time training on the overall Lead dataset, dancing with thousands of different Leads over the years, from beginning to advanced skill levels, and learning how Leads in general lead. This has allowed her to develop an advanced general-purpose following algorithm, which is then customized for each Lead as she dances with them and learns their quirks.

Therefore, if you want to get better at following, the best way to do so is to follow repeatedly. To get better at following in general, dance with many different Leads, and to get better at dancing with specific Leads, dance repeatedly with them. Of course, it's a good idea to take classes along the way as well, to learn the common vocabulary before being thrown into it, which will allow you to focus on the nuances of following, rather than just trying to keep your head above water.

∞

When Melissa first explained this analogy to Nick, he was struck not only by how much it resonated with his own experience as a Follow, but also by how much it resonated with his experience as a Lead.

The idea that following can be thought of as a physical form of autocomplete is relatively intuitive. But what if leading is the same thing?

Leading as Autocomplete

A naïve view of leading sees each variation as a free choice by the Lead. For example, at every primary cross-step, the Lead can choose to lead any one of the hundreds of Cross-Step Waltz variations that exist, right?

The idea that the Lead chooses whatever he wants to lead isn't wrong, per se. In fact, many Leads and Follows think about dancing this way. But there are two issues with this idea: 1) it's an incomplete description of what's really going on in most social dance partnerships, and 2) thinking about dancing in this way limits us and keeps us from reaching a greater potential.

So what is actually going on? An experienced Lead understands that he isn't actually choosing between hundreds of variations at each primary cross-step. Instead, he's making a choice between just a few different options that come to mind at the moment: options that are presented to him by his own version of autocomplete.

As an analogy, consider the following sentence:

Once upon a time, there was a _____.

Theoretically, any word could fill that blank. But some words are much more likely than others, because some words will make for a better sentence (and a better story).

First, we probably want to choose a word in English to avoid surprising the reader by mixing languages. Second, we want the sentence to be grammatically correct.

In social dancing, this is equivalent to first, leading something that's consistent with the current dance form and music, and second, leading something that's physically comfortable from where the Follow is. Already, this has reduced the number of possible choices dramatically.

In addition, you'll want to write a story your audience will understand. And perhaps most importantly, you'll want to write a story your audience wants to read. This is equivalent to leading something the Follow will understand how to follow, and something she'll enjoy dancing.

Based on these constraints (and many more, including not wanting to do the same thing seven times in a row, having adequate floor space, etc.), the Lead's autocomplete algorithm will present a few different options for his consideration, from which he'll choose one. That's how leading works in social dancing. Just as Follows aren't just "ready for anything," Leads don't actually choose from "anything," just a short list of logical possibilities.

So far, we've seen that just as Follows use a kind of autocomplete to follow, Leads also use a kind of autocomplete to choose the next variation to lead. But it turns out that as Leads we can take this even further, and choose the variation *while we're leading it*.

Letting It Evolve

For example, in Cross-Step Waltz, you can start with He Goes, then, *while you're going under*, decide what comes next: a turn, a free spin, a rollaway, etc. In our linguistic analogy, this is equivalent to typing the letters "pre" and then picking from the list of autocompleted words that start with those letters:

> press
> prefer
> prelude
> precious
> president

As a first iteration of this approach to leading, you can start with those three letters, and then, once you've identified your preferred ending for the word, press "enter" (so to speak) and lead the rest of it. For example, as you're leading "pre," see "precious," choose it, then lead the Follow into "cious." In physical terms, while leading He Goes, see the various She Goes options (Inside Turn, Free Spin, or Rollaway), choose the Inside Turn, then lead into it.

Whether they know it or not, most Leads have probably stumbled upon this approach at least occasionally, although perhaps in a slightly different way. As a Lead, you may notice that sometimes you intend to lead "precious," but, as you're dancing "pre," you have a better idea (a safer one, a more comfortable one, a more musical one, etc.), and switch, on the fly, to leading "press." Or perhaps you lead "pre," and the Follow dances "pref," leading you to adapt to leading "prefer." This is equivalent to switching to a Lead's Underarm Turn when there isn't enough space for She Goes, or making the most of things by dancing a Rollaway if she lets go and free spins herself when you were intending to lead an Inside Turn.

Dancing in the Moment

Experienced Leads might even experiment with applying this process to every step. For example, you might start by typing the letter "t" (perhaps equivalent to leading the first step of a Grapevine) and see what possibilities arise:

> talk
> texas
> tree
> tokyo

Tentatively choose "tree" (intending to lead a Six-Count Grapevine, Double Outside Turn), but don't press "enter" yet. Instead, just press "r" (continuing the grapevine) and see what new options come to mind:

> tree
> trade
> trillion
> trust

If you still like "tree" (the Double Turn) keep typing "tree" (finishing out the grapevine into the prep on 1). But if something else appeals to you more, switch on-the-fly to leading that instead. For example, you might switch to "trade" (a Five-Count Grapevine, Inside Turn and Outside Turn) by typing "a":

> trade
> track
> travel
> transfer

If you still like "trade," (the Five-Count Grapevine, Inside Turn and Outside Turn) keep going by typing "d":

> trade
> tradeoff
> trademark
> tradition

At this point, you can finish your currently intended variation by typing "e." Or you can keep going on to lead into a longer combination that has come to mind ("tradeoff", "trademark"), or continue the process of discovering what comes next step by step ("tradi___").

Attentive Leads base each of these choices on where their partner is at each moment, and which autocomplete options would work best for her.

Writing the Story as You Go

Beginners tend to approach leading from the opposite end of the spectrum. Rather than letting the current word evolve moment by moment, they're planning out the entire sentence, or paragraph. "First, I'll do two Turning Basics, then He Goes, She Goes, then three more Basics, and a Grapevine Outside Turn." Of course, we can't blame them—we've all been there, and know what it's like to worry that you won't know what to lead next.

But in Cross-Step Waltz, you don't need to stress about this. Instead, you can just focus on what you're currently leading, knowing that you can always come back to the Turning Basic, which is easy and endlessly satisfying, before you need to think about leading the next thing.

Wherever you are in your leading journey, we encourage you to move the needle just a little bit closer to dancing in the moment, co-authoring the story with the Follow as you go, rather than writing it all out long before she gets there.

The Bottom Line

In this chapter, we've seen that the ideal approaches to following and leading are less different than they may initially appear. In actuality, they're two sides of the same coin: two versions of autocomplete. Rather than the Follow being in the moment and the Lead thinking ahead, both are simultaneously in the moment and looking forward. While the Follow is in the moment, sensing the logical next step, the Lead is in the moment, finding and leading that same step.

Chapter 21

Pivot Variations

Some turning dances, like Schottische, Hambo, and Zwiefacher, are based on 180° pivot steps. Ever the chameleon, Cross-Step Waltz also incorporates variations based on pivots.

The most common pivot variations in Cross-Step Waltz begin with a Single Pivot:

Single Pivot

(1) The primary cross-step of a Turning Basic, but rotating more than usual.

(2) The Lead steps back L across LOD in front of the Follow, looking back at her and taking a squarer frame, as she steps R forward between his feet.

(3) Pivot halfway around, with the Follow backing L across LOD and the Lead stepping forward R between her feet.

On (1-2-3), you complete a full rotation, spinning twice as fast as you usually do (360° in three counts instead of the usual six).

(4) Both walk forward into the second half of one of the next few variations.

But first, here are some tips for more successful pivots:

- Face your partner more squarely than usual, heart-to-heart, with parallel shoulders.
- Sink down slightly lower. You'll be more stable with a lower center of gravity.
- Hang back from your partner, with a comfortable volume of space between you. This will help you gain leverage.
- The frame for pivots is firmer than the usual frame for a Turning Basic. You need that firmness in order to …
- Rotate more! Rotate yourself more, and help your partner rotate more, by hanging back in the frame and turning the core of your body CW. For both partners, but Leads es-

pecially, use your body to rotate your partner, rather than grappling with your hands. While pivots are necessarily physical, comfort is still paramount, and the ideal is to have your pivots feel as comfortable and easygoing as any other figure.

- *Leads*: Don't try to apply torque with your right hand, or you'll hurt your partner's back. Instead, keep your arm firmly connected to your body as if it's a tree limb, and assist your partner's rotation with a body lead through the whole frame, instead of applying pressure points.

- *Leads*: Make it extra clear you're pivoting. Your second step of a Single Pivot is basically in the same place as the second step of a Turning Basic, but everything that comes after is different, so make it clear to her that it's going to be different. Give her as many clues as you can: face her more squarely, sink lower, hang back, rotate more, and maybe give her that mischievous look and smile that says "Pivots!" When you're done pivoting, clearly lead back into a Turning Basic by slowing the rotation and returning to a slightly more relaxed frame.

- *Follows*: Your partner will appreciate all the help you can give him in these regards. When you feel any of the things above happening, respond in kind. For example, if he faces you more squarely, face him more squarely, and if he hangs back more, hang back more. For more on this, see "Active Following" on p. 111.

∞

While the Single Pivot is an important element, it isn't a complete variation by itself. Once you've mastered it, you can use it as an entrance into the following variations:

Pivot Outside Turn [POT]

(1-2-3) "Cross-pivot-pivot" as described in the Single Pivot.

(4-5-6) A Follow's outside turn in the outside lane. The Follow pivots forward, back, forward under the arm while the Lead walks forward three steps. Make sure the Follow is facing forward along LOD in the outside lane at the beginning of the turn.

Follows: In this and other turns, you can make it easier for your partner to keep up with you if you take small steps, focusing more on rotating to face forward, back, forward rather than traveling three large steps along LOD.

Leads: If you don't make it around in time to have the Follow facing forward in the outside lane on (4), don't force her into a turn. Instead, simply finish with three counts of Waltz Walk. If you make it dramatic, like a movie Tango promenade, it'll seem like it was intentional instead of a "mistake."

This can also be a **Pivot Free Spin** [PFS]. In this case, the Lead releases the Follow's right hand a moment early, on (3), to signal the free spin. But that release isn't necessarily a clear-enough cue that a free spin is coming, so it's the Lead's responsibility to make sure the Follow's left hand doesn't get caught on his back. (Good Follows will often move their hands further onto his back to help him through the pivot.) He can do this by lowering his shoulder and arm out of the way of her arm, rather than expecting her to lift her arm in time.

It can also be a **Pivot Rollaway** [PRW] or **Pivot Parallel Spin** [PPS].

∞

Chained Pivot Turns [CPV]

Chain two or more of the previous four variations in a row.

Chained Pivot Rollaways [CRO] are especially fun.

Intensifying Pivot Turns [IPT] are also fun. Intensifying means that each turn builds on the previous one, for example, a Pivot Outside Turn followed by a Pivot Free Spin followed by a Pivot Rollaway (or Pivot Parallel Spin).

∞

Texas Tommy [TEX]

The footwork and partnering of this move are the same as the Pivot Free Spin. The arms originally came from the early 20th century Apache (two syllables, rhymes with "squash"), and were later seen in the early ancestor to swing dancing, the Texas Tommy. Today, they're commonly seen in West Coast Swing (the Apache Whip) and Lindy Hop (the Texas Tommy).

While pivoting, the Lead takes the Follow's right hand (in his left), and places it into his right hand, comfortably low behind her back. (Follows, you can help determine where that is.) Then he gently rolls her off his right arm, similar to the Pivot Free Spin, but keeping right-in-right hands. Leads, whatever you do, don't pull on her right hand! Instead, gently guide her into her continued rotation with your right arm (not your hand).

See what you can do from this right-in-right handhold. Perhaps a right-in-right Grapevine Free Spin (p. 45), a right-in-right Halo Frisbee (p. 28), or a right-in-right Flip to Shadow (p. 137). Or you can simply pass her right hand back into his left and recommence a Turning Basic, as shown in the video.

∞

Tripled Single Pivots [TSP]

This is an all-time favorite.

Three Single Pivots in a row, for a total of 12 counts. "Cross-pivot-pivot-walk" x 4.

You'll temporarily be off the music (dancing four against three), but that gives you the satisfaction of getting back on the music at the end of the figure.

Pivots to Fix the Timing [PFT]

A succession of Single Pivots can also be used to shift the downbeat and get you back on the timing. The following table illustrates where the downbeat will end up after one, two, and three Single Pivots when started on the count on the left. The downbeats you're aiming for (1 and 4) are highlighted in gray.

	One Pivots	Two Pivots	Three Pivots
Ct. 1	5	3	1
Ct. 2	6	4	2
Ct. 3	1	5	3
Ct. 4	2	6	4
Ct. 5	3	1	5
Ct. 6	4	2	6

While we're providing this table for your interest, we don't recommend you actually use it: instead, if you're dancing on the 2, 3, 5, or 6, just keep doing Single Pivots (one or two of them) until you end up on the 1 or 4. Note that to shift from one downbeat to the other (i.e., from 4 to 1), you'll need to use another method, like Stop and Go (p. 20).

∞

Pivots to Finish the Phrase [PFP]

This useful innovation is from Lilli Ann and Claire Carey.

If you're on the correct foot, but somehow end up with three extra counts in closed position at the end of a phrase, you can finish out the phrase with a pivot: the Lead backs L across LOD as the Follow steps forward R between his feet (4), the Follow backs L across LOD as the Lead steps forward R between her feet (5), and both walk along LOD (6).

As long as it's led comfortably, it's much more satisfying than just "walking it out."

The video shows an example of the Lead accidentally sweeping the Follow across LOD on (2) then finishing the phrase with a pivot.

∞

Delayed Pivot Recovery [DPR]

The same idea can also be used as a recovery when spontaneous improvisation leaves the Follow unable to recommence a Turning Basic on (1). Rather than forcing it, just walk for two counts, then do a Single Pivot:

(1-2) Waltz Walk along LOD for two steps, stabilizing an uncertain outcome.

(3-4-5-6) A Single Pivot: "cross-pivot-pivot-walk."

Follow's Grapevine to Delayed Pivot Recovery [GDP]

Specifically, after spontaneous improvisation, the Follow is often crossing behind on (1). Here is a smooth recovery:

(1) The Follow crosses behind as the Lead crosses in front.

(2) Step side along LOD as the he starts leading her to cross in front on (3).

(3) The Follow crosses in front as the Lead crosses in front again.

(4-5-6) Pivot-pivot-walk.

If you want to practice, we recommend you do it in action, not starting cold with the Follow crossing behind on (1). The easiest exercise is:

(1-6) A long Six-Step Grapevine.

(1-6) Follow's Grapevine to Delayed Pivot Recovery.

∞

Joining the Follow for Pivots [JFP]

The above concept can also be used to join the Follow for pivots at the end of a variation that otherwise ends in a Follow's outside turn on (4-5-6).

For example, lead into a Six-Count Grapevine, Double Outside Turn (p. 47), catching her in waltz position between the two turns to join her for a partnered pivot instead of the second turn. Or try a Cross-Body Inside Turn to Pivaloop (p. 29) into a Pivot, as shown in the video.

∞

Free Spin to Pivots, Outside Turn [FPO]

Here's another variation in which he joins her in the middle of pivots.

(1-2-3) The Lead sends the Follow across into the inside lane with a low-hand cross-body lead to swingout position.

(4-5-6) The Lead sends the Follow across into the outside lane with a CW free spin, as the Follow steps cross (i.e., forward to the outside wall), back, forward.

(1) The Lead steps forward R toward the Follow, catching in closed position for a Follow-backing pivot with the Follow's back toward the outside wall. Pivot 90° CW together into:

(2-3) A full CW pivot along LOD, Lead backing (2), then Follow backing (3).

(4-5-6) A Follow's outside turn along LOD.

Sweep to Pivots, Outside Turn and Free Spin [SPF]

This variation has the same parts as the previous one, in a different order, with the free spin at the end instead of in the middle.

(1-2-3) The Lead sends the Follow across into the inside lane with a low-hand cross-body lead to swingout position.

(4) The Lead sweeps the Follow across LOD in front of him (without a free spin).

(5) The Lead steps forward R toward the Follow, catching in closed position for a Follow-backing pivot with the Follow's back toward the outside wall. Pivot 90° CW together into:

(6-1) A full CW pivot along LOD, Lead backing (6), then Follow backing (1).

(2-3) A Follow's outside turn, the Follow stepping forward, back.

(4-5-6) A Follow's free spin, the Follow stepping forward, back, forward.

This could also be a **Sweep to Pivots, Double Outside Turn** or a **Sweep to Pivots, Outside Turn and Rollaway**.

Some find this family of variations a little easier than the previous one, since the lead hands are already connected leading into the first pivot step on (5), whereas in the previous variation, you catch for pivots straight out of a free spin. But they're all good, when led clearly.

Either version can be substituted for any Follow's sweep across LOD on (4-5-6), as in He Goes, She Goes (and many other variations).

∞

For advanced dancers, multiple complete pivots can be strung together in sequence:

Double Pivots [DBP]

Two full pivots in six counts: "cross-pivot-pivot-pivot-pivot-walk."

This can also be done pivoting in place, with easygoing "baby pivots," completing one full rotation in six counts rather than two.

∞

Quintuple Pivots [QTP]

Five full pivots in twelve counts: "cross, 10 pivot steps, walk."

This is usually done in place, without traveling, but advanced dancers sometimes travel with it.

The next two variations mix dynamic pivots with a dramatic stop, for a nice juxtaposition:

Pivot Catch [PVC]

Richard came up with this one while playing around with variations after one of his Saint Petersburg classes, inspired by one of Georgiy "Rold" Shulpin's variations.

(1-2-3) An easygoing "cross-pivot-pivot," which is so easygoing that the Follow is backing R along LOD on (4), in front of the Lead.

(4) The Lead faces forward along LOD and catches the Follow, stopping her.

(5) Without moving the feet, rock the Lead back/side against LOD as the Follow rocks forward/side against LOD. During this step, the Lead begins to rotate the Follow CW to face forward along LOD.

(6) Both step along LOD in preparation for the primary cross-step.

In addition to being fun, this also functions as a safe recovery if you start pivoting but find you don't have enough space to safely turn the Follow or keep pivoting.

∞

Brake Step [BRK]

This is a similar variation from Nick and Melissa, but inverting the stop and the pivot. This figure also has a purpose: to immediately protect the Follow when you're about to crash into something. The Lead literally "takes the blow" with his back. But it's mostly just done for fun, not necessarily to prevent a crash.

(1) The usual primary cross-step.

(2) The Lead backs around in front of the Follow and stops, blocking her travel along LOD.

(3) Rock onto the other foot, against LOD.

(4-5-6) Finish with a single pivot: Lead backs along LOD (4), Follow backs along LOD (5), and both step along LOD (6).

Once stopped, the pivots on (4) and (5) allow you to travel around an obstacle: rotate more to pass to the outside of the obstruction, or rotate less to pass to the inside.

∞

Coda Pivot

While most pivot variations start with the Lead backing, this one starts with the Follow backing. The name "Coda" is borrowed from the world of music, referring to something added to the end, as this pivot is.

(1-2-3-4) The first four counts of a Turning Basic.

(5) The Follow backs L in front of the Lead, as he steps forward R between her feet.

(6) The Lead backs L in front of the Follow, completing the pivot. The Lead is now in the outside lane, which can lead to several outcomes.

∞

Coda Pivot to Inside Turn [CPI]

(1-6) Coda Pivot, releasing the elbows-side connection at the end while slowing down the Follow's CW rotation, to prepare for a slower CCW rotation in the next bar. The key is to set her up for—and clearly lead her into—a step straight forward along LOD in the inside lane on the next (1).

(1-6) Let go of the elbows-side connection, along LOD, and clearly lead into the second half of He Goes, She Goes (p. 33), i.e., the Follow does an inside turn on the inside lane (1-2-3), and then sweeps across LOD to closed position (4-5-6).

As the second half of this is the same as the second half of He Goes, She Goes, anything that modifies or comes out of the second half of He Goes, She Goes can modify or come out of a Coda Pivot to Inside Turn.

∞

Coda Pivot to Outside Turn and Free Spin [CPO]

When led clearly, the previous variation is a satisfying surprise, but this version is easier to lead and follow, since it continues the Follow's CW momentum, rather than redirecting her.

(1-6) Coda Pivot.

(1-6) An outside turn and free spin, like a Pivaloop Free Spin (p. 29), but from closed position. It starts with a third, Follow-backing pivot step across LOD into the "Pivaloop" part of the turn.

∞

Reverse pivots, which turn CCW instead of CW, are also possible. Here are a few variations involving reverse pivots:

Reverse Pivot to Follow's Lunge [RPL]

This is the variation from Georgiy "Rold" Shulpin that inspired Richard's Pivot Catch (p. 107). This one has a left pivot in place of the right pivot.

(1-2) A cross-body lead into a reverse pivot, Follow backing on (2).

(3) Continue the reverse pivot with the Lead backing.

(4) Catch the Follow in a lunge straight along LOD. (In this version, there isn't really enough time for this to feel like a lunge—it's more like a block or a rock—but we'll call it a lunge to be consistent with the next variation.)

(5) Rock the Follow back out of it against LOD.

(6) Both step along LOD.

∞

Reverse Pivot to Hesitating Lunge and Pivot [RHL]

Richard mentioned to Nick and Melissa that it feels more natural to hold the lunge on (4), instead of rushing out of it. This means you're still rebounding from the lunge on (1-2) of the next bar. In response, they passed on Lilli Ann and Claire Carey's suggestion (p. 104) of filling out an extra bar of music with a single pivot. Notice the community of six contributors (from four cities in two countries) that created this variation.

(1-2-3-4) Do the above Reverse Pivot into Follow's Lunge.

(5-6) Hold the lunge.

(1-2-3) Slowly rock out of the lunge, against LOD. The Lead begins to rotate CW in front of the Follow on (3).

(4-5) A single CW pivot starting with the Lead's L backing around in front of Follow's R.

(6) Walk forward out of the pivot, both facing along LOD.

∞

Though reverse pivots are relatively rare in social dancing, there are some particularly nice Foxtrot variations based on them. Knowing this, Nick and Melissa challenged each other to adapt some of these variations into Cross-Step Waltz. Here are the results:

Chassé Molinete [CHM]

This is Nick's adaptation of the left-turning rocking step in Foxtrot, which is also seen in Tango and Kizomba. Like Tripled Single Pivots, it's a twelve-count variation in which you temporarily dance across the music.

(1) Primary cross-step, with the Follow winning the race along LOD, starting to turn CCW.

(2-3-4-5) Rock the Follow back along LOD (2), rock the Lead back against LOD (3), and side-close toward the hands (4-5). You turn about 2/3 of a rotation CCW in these four steps, pivoting on the spot. The Follow's side-close on (4-5) is larger than the Lead's, as she traces out a CCW circle around him while he stays mostly in place.

(6-7-8-9) Repeat the last four counts, again turning 2/3 of a rotation CCW.

(10-11-12) One final rocking reverse pivot 2/3 CCW, finishing the second full rotation (10-11), then step side/forward along LOD (12) to prepare for a primary cross-step.

∞

Park Avenue with Pivots [PAV]

This is Melissa's adaptation of the popular Park Avenue with Pivots, which is one of our students' all-time favorite Foxtrot steps. It's also danced across the music in twelve counts.

(1-2-3-4) A Single Pivot: cross (1), pivot (2), pivot (3), then both step side along LOD (4).

(5) Back the Lead one step straight into the center of the room, with Lead's R and Follow's L.

(6-7-8) A single reverse pivot that starts by backing the Follow. The Follow backs across LOD (6), the Lead backs across LOD (7), and both step side along LOD (8).

(9) Back the Follow one step straight toward the outside wall, with Lead's R and Follow's L.

(10-11-12) A regular pivot that starts by backing the Lead: Lead backs across LOD (10), Follow backs across LOD (11), and both walk along LOD (12) to prepare for a primary cross-step.

This one is easiest to parse if you think of it as "get ready, pivot, pivot, side" x 3. The "get ready" is first a cross with the first foot, then backing the Lead on the first foot, then backing the Follow on the first foot.

Chapter 22

Active Following

When we ask Leads what distinguishes their favorite partners, the responses can generally be summed up as, "Everything just works when I'm dancing with her. Even when I lead something that doesn't work with anyone else, she makes it flow effortlessly. I don't know how, but she makes me a better dancer."

Follows, you want to be this "her." But how exactly? In this chapter, we'll share many practical tips for achieving this, but first, we need to deconstruct a common myth.

"Just following."

When asked how they follow, many Follows we've talked to over the years have given the same reply: "Oh, I'm just following." This phrase, Melissa's least favorite phrase in the world, reveals a lack of ownership of the dance, in both its positive and negative qualities. It means that whatever good things happen in the dance—like perfect execution of a series of difficult figures—the Lead gets all the credit because the Follow was "just following." And whatever bad things may happen in the dance—like slamming into another couple—the Lead takes all the blame because the Follow was "just following." Rather than being an equal partner, "just following" means the Follow is no more than an instrument that the Lead uses to create his own work of art, the quality for which he is solely responsible.

This isn't how dancing actually works. While it's true that the Lead is mostly responsible for selecting the figures, the Lead and Follow have an equal responsibility for executing them, and get equal credit for the corresponding parts they play in making them work. And while it's also true that the Lead is responsible for not spinning the Follow into another couple, both partners should be aware of the other couples around them. Rather than just being an instrument, the Follow is an equal partner in the dance.

But what exactly does the Follow's role in this equal partnership look like?

Physical Connection

In leading and following, there are two different kinds of forces involved: tension (i.e., pulling), and compression (i.e., pushing). While the Lead often initiates these forces, the Follow is an equal partner in creating them.

For example, if the Lead hangs back in the frame to lead a pivot, the Follow hangs back with equal and opposite force (tension), allowing them to easily swing each other by. And if the Lead pushes into the Follow's hand to lead a free spin, the Follow pushes back with equal and opposite force (compression), allowing her to push off into the free spin.

In both of these cases, and many more, it's physically impossible for the Lead to create the required forces by himself: he needs active help from the Follow. For example, if she doesn't hang back in the pivot, the Lead hanging back will simply pull her toward him. And if she doesn't push back into his hand for the free spin, her hand will simply flop down beside her.

The more active the Follow is in this force-balancing, the easier leading and following become, and the more enjoyable the dance is for both roles.

∞

Interpretation and Amplification

As we've often said in our classes, even though the Lead usually initiates a turn, the Follow gets the credit for it. There are several different reasons for this.

First, there's nothing about a halo over your head that inherently means "turn." Often, at a non-dance event, we'll see a husband trying to lead a turn while his wife is just standing there, letting her hand circle her head, without turning. Social dancing has its own (physical) language: to dance effectively, both partners need to understand the signals.

This is one reason why Follows take social dance classes. Just as Leads need to learn how to signal each kind of variation, Follows need to learn how to interpret these signals. So while the Lead gets some credit for giving the signals, the Follow gets even more credit for the greater challenge of interpreting those signals.

In addition to getting credit for interpreting the Lead's signals, the Follow also gets credit for amplifying them. A good Lead doesn't crank the Follow through a turn: instead, he simply suggests it by drawing a halo. The turning itself is provided by the Follow.

This is true for more than just turns. Whatever signals the Lead provides, the Follow amplifies them, taking a small movement made by the Lead and turning it into something much bigger. The Lead makes a small halo, and the Follow does a whole turn. The Lead rotates a bit more, and the Follow helps them do a full pivot. The Lead pushes his right shoulder forward slightly, and she turns her body CCW to cross L behind.

As a Follow, the more of this kind of amplification you do (within reason), the easier the Lead will find it to lead you, and the more you'll be able to do as a couple.

∞

Co-Navigation

Some traveling dances, like One Step, are based on backing the Follow along LOD. In dances like these, navigation is entirely up to the Lead because he's the only one who can see where they're going. And in general, navigation is considered to be the Lead's responsibility.

But in Cross-Step Waltz, the Follow is usually facing forward on each primary cross-step, and can see where the couple is heading. Probably toward that open space on the right, not into that crowd of dancers on the left. So the Follow senses that her partner is guiding them toward the open space, and helps them both flow in that direction.

The Lead appreciates this help from the Follow, even if he doesn't know he's being helped ("I don't know why, but it just works better with her!").

Here's an exercise we often use to demonstrate this. The Lead picks a spot on the floor about two Turning Basics' distance away, but doesn't tell the Follow where it is. Then he tries to navigate them to that spot on the floor. Next, the Lead and Follow confer and mutually agree on a different spot on the floor, again, about two Turning Basics away. Now, they co-navigate to that spot. Everyone finds it much easier when the Follow is helping.

At a social dance, the Follow doesn't know exactly where the Lead is intending to go, but this doesn't mean she can't help with navigation.

First, even if you have no idea where you're going as a Follow, you can tune into the Lead's navigational cues and amplify them. If he's turning you more, turn him more. If he's turning you less, turn him less. Even if the Lead doesn't notice you're doing it, he'll appreciate how much easier it is to navigate with you.

Second, you can actually help him decide where to go. In a crowded room, the Lead will probably be looking to go toward the open space in order to have more room for variations. Therefore, you too can be on the lookout for open space, and gently guide him in that direction, particularly in the moments when you can see and he can't, e.g., when he's backing around on the first half of a Turning Basic.

This is especially important if you notice that you're going to crash. If you think the crash can be avoided through evasive maneuvers, gently guide him away from it. But sometimes, you'll just need to bring him to a full stop. In either case, most Leads will thank you for saving them. (The ones who bark "Who's leading here?!" don't deserve to have you as a partner.)

∞

Making It Work

"Even when I lead something that doesn't work with anyone else, it flows effortlessly with her." Why is that? His partner is actively helping him in a way that his other partners are not.

When first-day beginners dance with each other, it's often like the blind leading the blind. But when the same beginning Leads dance with Melissa, everything works perfectly, like magic. Of course, it isn't actually magic. It's that Melissa is actively helping from the Follow role.

For example, in a Turning Basic, if he's not winning the race on (1), she'll gently push him ahead of her. Similarly, on (2), if he's not getting all the way across LOD, she'll gently sweep him into the proper position. Then, on the second half, she'll actively send herself by, even if he isn't giving her any help.

Similarly, if she knows he's trying to lead a particular variation, she'll dance it perfectly (and help him dance it perfectly), even if he isn't leading it perfectly. ("Wow, that was the first time that ever worked!")

As an experienced Follow, in all but the most creative cases, Melissa has a good idea of what the Lead is intending, even if he doesn't lead it very well. Therefore, even when the signals aren't quite right, she can still correctly interpret and amplify them. And not only that, she often has enough mental capacity left over to help him through his part as well!

Returning to our autocomplete analogy in Chapter 20, Melissa and other Follows like her are using not only an autocomplete algorithm, but an autocomplete algorithm with autocorrect!

It's important to note that the approach we're describing here is completely different from back-leading. Back-leading is when the Follow takes over and starts leading (in particular, choosing the figures). "Making it work," on the other hand, means seeing the Lead's vision, however cloudy that vision might be, and helping him bring it to life by doing your part (and maybe even helping him do his). While Leads generally dislike back-leading, they generally love when you do this.

Now, as a Follow, you may well say "I can't do that," or "I don't want to do that." In the latter case, that's your prerogative, but we'd highly encourage you to reconsider, as it will raise your dancing (and your partners' dancing) to even greater heights, and make you one of the most desirable partners. In the former case, you absolutely can do this. In fact, we often encourage Follows to do it in the Turning Basic on their very first day of Cross-Step Waltz, using the techniques we mentioned above.

Active Attention

In order to do all of the above, you need to be actively paying attention to all of the signals you're receiving. In other words, you want to have "all of your antennae open."

One of your antennae should be tuned into the physical cues you're receiving. Pay close attention to the points of contact between you and your partner, whether it's palm to palm, hand to back, or fingertip to fingertip. The more carefully you're monitoring for subtle changes in those points of contact, the earlier you'll know what's likely to happen next.

Another antenna should be monitoring for visual clues. Where is the Lead looking? Where is there open space? Where is his body relative to yours? All of these visual cues (and more) can help you further narrow down what's likely to come.

In addition to physical and visual cues, you can also tune into auditory cues. As we noted in Chapter 15, by listening carefully to the music, you'll be able to sense when a musical Lead will be most likely to lead something, and be especially attentive then. In addition, you can help him dance musically by physically amplifying the music, starting by helping him step right on the beat. Finally, by listening carefully, you'll also be able to catch any verbal leads, whether intentional (a helpful cue to "lunge"), or unintentional (concerned noises that indicate danger and a desire to be helped with navigation).

Of the five traditional senses, active Follows have three—touch, sight, and hearing—fully engaged. But humans actually have more than five senses, of which active Follows have two additional senses fully engaged: proprioception (sense of body position and movement as measured by neurons in your muscles and joints), and equilibrioception (sense of angular and linear acceleration and balance as measured by your inner ear).

Therefore, rather than tuning out and "just following," see how fully you can tune into all five of these senses at once. The more engaged you are in the moment, the easier it will be to follow, and the more you'll be able to do as a couple.

∞

Adding Your Own Style

If Follows were truly "just following," and everything were up to the Lead to decide, there wouldn't be any reason for him to dance with different partners, since his experience would be the same each time. Fortunately, this isn't the case.

Each partner, and thus, each dance, is unique. Just as two skilled musicians will have different interpretations of the same piece of music, two skilled Follows will have different interpretations of the same variation. This is one of the reasons that Leads do like to dance with different partners over the course of an evening. Even if they dance the exact same variations each time, the experience will be different with different partners.

One of the qualities that distinguishes the best Follows is that they have the ability to bring their own unique style to the dance, which influences and inspires the Lead and elevates their combined dancing far beyond the rote remembrance of steps. The best Follows don't "just follow," they *dance!* And in doing so, they inspire the Lead to *dance*, rather than just leading a sequence of moves.

In a purely social dance like Cross-Step Waltz (as opposed to competition and exhibition dances), there isn't one right or wrong way to do this. Your style is your own, and no one is going to police it. But your partners will appreciate it when you bring your own unique style to the dance, rather than just relying on them to do everything. Allow your personality to shine through!

∞

Owning It

Even if you aren't entirely sure what's going on, go confidently into the unknown, rather than constantly second-guessing yourself. Whether it's in adding your own style, or interpreting the Lead's signals, whatever you do, totally own it.

Keep moving in the direction that your informed instinct seems to indicate, as you keep time with your feet under your body. While this easy piece of advice seems like it would be far too simple to actually function, the vast majority of the time, your body will make it work, even if your mind isn't sure what's going on. In fact, this technique sometimes works even when the Lead has no idea what's going on either ("I didn't think that was going to work, but whatever you did saved us!").

∞

Expressing Yourself

Some Follows have been trained, through other dance forms like competition or exhibition dance, to maintain a certain kind of facial expression while dancing. In social dancing, however, you're free to express yourself however you want.

For example, if you're enjoying something, let it show! Leads of all experience levels tell us that even if a Follow isn't the most experienced dancer, as long as she's having fun, she's fun to dance with. In addition to knowing that you're having fun in general, Leads also appreciate knowing what kinds of variations you find most fun, so they can lead more like those.

On the other hand, if you're not enjoying something (e.g., if something is uncomfortable), you can let that show too. Just as Leads appreciate knowing what you like, they also appreciate knowing what you don't like so they can avoid doing it again.

Of course, these are also things you can express verbally, telling your Lead what you do and don't like, or giving them a heads-up that you have an injury. The more you communicate with your partner about what works and what doesn't, the easier it will be for both of you.

∞

Asking for a Dance

There's one more way to be an active Follow: don't be afraid to ask someone for a dance. It isn't the nineteenth century anymore. Anyone can ask to dance with anyone. So don't be shy, just ask someone for a dance!

"Social dancing is human contact
that allows you to touch
what your partner is thinking."

— Saloni Sanwalka,
Stanford social dancer

Chapter 23

Cradle Position Variations

Cradle Position, also called Sweetheart or Cuddle, is an open two-hand inside turn. It's a common position in many social dances, including Cross-Step Waltz. We use the term Cradle because it's the most unambiguous name for this position.

∞

Cradle Position

From open two-hands, the Lead lowers his right hand and leads the Follow into an inside turn with his left hand, bringing the left-to-right hands into the frame, continuing to hold both hands. The Follow turns CCW and backs into the Lead's right arm. The Lead then lowers his left arm to a comfortable level in front of the Follow. Both are facing the same direction at the end, with the Follow at the Lead's right.

∞

Entrances to Cradle Position

Inside Turn to Cradle [ITC]

This is the most common way of getting into Cradle Position. It's simply the beginning of Chained Inside and Outside Turns (p. 27), without the Outside Turn part.

(1) A non-rotating cross-step along LOD.

(2-3-4) The Lead rotates the Follow CCW and brings the held hands into the frame for an inside turn on (2). As she turns, he catches the rear hands (Lead's right to Follow's left), ending in Cradle Position facing along LOD, with the Follow at the Lead's right. She pivots back (2), forward (3), and walks forward (4). Note the delayed timing for the hand coming through the frame, on (2).

Leads: Make an extra effort to catch your partner's left hand with your right hand on (2), to take both hands for Cradle Position. It's easy to let her left hand escape, and difficult to recover it once it does.

(5-6) Continue to Waltz Walk forward along LOD in Cradle Position.

∞

Cross-Body Inside Turn to Cradle Wheel [CIC]

This is similar to the first entrance, except the Lead sends the Follow across to the inside lane on the inside turn on (2), catching in Cradle Position on (3) and leading the Follow to walk forward CCW around him until they're both facing LOD (4-5-6).

∞

Walkaround Wrap to Cradle [WWC]

Another easy way to get into Cradle Position is to begin a Turning Basic, then as the Lead passes in front of the Follow, looking back at her, his right hand slips from her shoulder blade to catch her left hand (1-2-3). He keeps his left hand in front of her, using both hands to help her continue to travel straight forward along LOD, as he circumnavigates her CW, ending with both facing forward along LOD in Cradle Position, the Lead at the Follow's left side (4-5-6).

Essentially, the Lead walks CW around the Follow, wrapping her up with open two-hands, as she continues to walk forward along LOD.

∞

He Goes to Cradle [HGC]

(1-2-3) He Goes (p. 33), passing under his left arm and in front of her to the outside lane.

(4-5-6) He offers his right hand to her left under the arch of the left-to-right hands and leads her to walk diagonally forward across LOD in front of him into Cradle position, as he passes behind her into the inside lane.

Both partners face forward along LOD the whole time, without turning.

Exits from Cradle Position

Outside Turn Exit from Cradle [OTC]

(1-2-3) Just Waltz Walk in Cradle. This delay is important. If you lead the outside turn on (1), the Follow's R isn't free, and there's too much time for a satisfying single turn.

(4-5-6) The Lead raises his left arm and circles the Follow's head once CW (an outside turn).

During the turn, either let go of right-to-left hands to retake waltz position for a Turning Basic, or keep the two-hand hold, for one of the many figures that utilizes that handhold.

∞

Roll-Off-the-Arm Exit from Cradle [RAC]

(1-2-3) Just Waltz Walk in Cradle.

(4-5-6) The Lead releases his left hand, and with his right arm, leads the Follow to turn once CW, keeping inside hands (her left in his right) at the end. The beauty of this is that there are many variations you can do from holding rear hands, and this is an elegant way to get them.

Leads: To lead this rolling off the arm, gently impart rotation with the part of your arm that's touching her back, rather than trying to lead it by pulling with your right hand, which would uncomfortably wrench her left arm.

∞

Double Outside Turn Exit from Cradle [DOC]

(1) Just walk in Cradle. The Follow's R isn't free yet.

(2-3-4-5-6) Letting go of the right-to-left hands, the Lead raises his left arm to lead a double outside turn for the Follow, with his left hand drawing two halos over her head. The Follow pivots CW along LOD, forward (2), back (3), forward (4), back (5), forward (6), catching in waltz position at the end.

It could also be an **Outside Turn and Free Spin Exit from Cradle**, or an **Outside Turn and Rollaway Exit from Cradle**.

Outside and Inside Turn Exit from Cradle [OIC]

(1) Just walk in Cradle.

(2-3) The Lead circles the Follow's head once with his left hand for a turn under left-to-right hands (an outside turn), keeping the right-to-left hands.

(4-5-6) Then he releases his left hand, and raises his right hand to circle the Follow's head a second time, but with right-to-left hands (an inside turn).

You end holding rear hands (his right and her left) with the Follow in the outside lane. There are many variations that can be done from this rear handhold, or you can just let go and catch your partner on the fly in waltz position.

∞

Deney Terrio Double Unwind Exit from Cradle [DTC]

Deney Terrio choreographed John Travolta's dances in *Saturday Night Fever*, and this is one of his disco moves, the Cuddle Spin. It's the same as above, except that the first turn is a Roll-Off-the-Arm.

The Lead releases left-to-right hands in front and leads the Follow to roll forward off his right arm for the first turn, then turn under the same arm for the second turn.

This will also leave you holding the rear hands, which you can use to lead a variety of figures, such as a Rear-Hand Grapevine Free Spin (p. 45), or Rear-Hand Face Loop (p. 45).

∞

Matador Around the World Exit from Cradle [DTM]

An outside turn under the high hands on (2-3), keeping the low hands held low, then another outside turn under the high hands on (4-5-6), allowing the low hands to wrap comfortably low behind her back into Matador position (p. 51).

Finish with a Matador Around the World or Matador Wheel (p. 52).

∞

Tornado Exit from Cradle [TFC]

Every other count, the Follow is set up to start the same kind of turn, so if we move the lead on (2) back two counts to the previous (6), that also works, and sets us up for this fancy exit.

(1-2-3-4-5) Waltz Walk in Cradle.

(6-1) The Lead raises the left-to-right hands to turn the Follow under, while keeping the right-to-left hands. She pivots forward, back.

(2-3) He keeps his left hand raised over her head as his right hand turns her a second time, under both sets of arms, as she pivots forward, back again. The secret is make a halo over her head with his right hand just *under* his raised left hand. Imagine that his left hand is a storm cloud, and his right is a tornado. This will give you crossed hands.

(4-5-6) The Lead leads the Follow to walk CW around him, as he do-si-dos CW around her to make it easier for her.

(1-6) A two-handed Pivaloop Free Spin (p. 29), which resolves the crossed hands. The final free spin could also be a rollaway.

∞

Cradle Release Exit [CRE]

If you raise the upper (left-to-right) hands in Cradle, you already have the held hands of waltz position. Therefore, if you let go of the left-to-right hands that are wrapped around her, you can lead straight into most variations in Cross-Step Waltz. For example, you can lead an inside turn on (2) into any variation that starts that way, or the Lead can dive under into He Goes. Or you can simply lead into a Turning Basic, as the Lead's right arm rises to her left shoulder and the Follow's left arm sneaks up between them to his right shoulder, in waltz position.

The video shows a Cross-Body Inside Turn to Pivaloop Free Spin straight out of Cradle.

∞

Variations in Cradle Position

Cradle Walk [CWK]

Simply walk forward in Cradle Position.

∞

Cradle Wheel [CRW]

In Cradle Position, lead the Follow forward as the Lead backs up, turning CCW as a couple.

Note that the wheel turns mostly on the spot, with the axis between the partners, rather than rolling along LOD.

Chained Cradle [CHC]

From Cradle Position, exit with an outside turn on (4-5-6), but keep both hands.

Then the Lead passes in front of the Follow to the outside lane, breaking through the left-to-right hands as in a waist slide while leading the Follow to pass behind his back with his raised right hand, which he's passing under. Then he leads the Follow to pass in front of him under his raised left hand, as she does exactly what he did (and vice versa).

If you know Chained Inside Turns or Loop-de-Loops from another dance, this is the same thing, just traveling forward along LOD. If not, the video will help you clarify the maneuver.

You can either alternate who's passing in front every three counts (as shown in the video), or if you're not quite making it, just walk through it using as many counts as it takes to get around your partner comfortably.

To get out of it, simply stop doing it, either catching the Follow in Cradle Position, or catching her in waltz position in time for a Turning Basic on (1).

There are also many other ways to exit from Chained Cradle, but they all depend on where you happen to be in terms of the figure and the music, so you'll need to play it by ear and see what's comfortable to lead at that moment.

∞

Cradle Yo Yo [CYY]

(1-2-3) Just Waltz Walk in Cradle.

(4-5-6) Release the left-to-right hands and roll the Follow off the Lead's right arm into the outside lane.

(1-2-3) Roll the Follow in, winding her up along the Lead's right arm to return to Cradle.

You can also use just the first half to get from Cradle to right-to-left hands, or the second half to get from right-to-left hands to Cradle.

∞

Inside Turn to Cradle Lunge [ICL]

(1-2-3) From closed position, an inside turn into Cradle Position, bringing the hands through the frame on (2).

(4-5-6) In Cradle Position, both lunge forward onto the outside foot (4), with inside knees approaching the floor, but carefully, to avoid bruising your kneecaps (5-6).

Leads: Don't drag the Follow down to the floor! Instead, think "land the plane" between (3) and (4), gently gliding down forward onto the runway, rather than dragging her straight down (or worse, backwards).

(1-2-3) Rise, shifting weight back against LOD, not forward.

(4-5-6) Outside turn exit, beginning on the outside feet.

Hint: This variation can be assisted with a verbal lead, the Lead whispering "lunge" during the inside turn. By the time the Follow processes what he means, she'll be doing it.

This can either be done at a musical moment in the middle of a dance, or as elegant way to end a dance (p. 156).

∞

Cradle Whip [CWH]

This variation was invented by participants at Austin Waltz Weekend 2014, based on a Cradle Whip in West Coast Swing.

(1-2-3-4) The first four counts of a Turning Basic.

(5-6) The Lead sends the Follow straight back diagonally along LOD toward the outside wall, slipping away to open two-hands, redirecting her momentum back toward him on (6).

(1-2) The Lead leads the Follow straight forward by his right side, wrapping her into Cradle position with his left hand as he rotates CW on the spot to face against LOD, and redirecting her momentum back along LOD on (2).

(3-4-5-6) The Lead sends the Follow straight back by his right side, diagonally along LOD toward the outside wall. When she reaches his right arm, they let go of right-to-left hands and slide back into waltz position for a Turning Basic on the next (1).

Leads: After the first four counts of Turning Basic, be sure to impart no rotation at all throughout the rest of the figure.

Follows: In general, but particularly in this figure, if you don't feel any rotation, don't rotate.

Once you've perfected the Cradle Whip, you can up the ante with a **Shoulder Whip** [SHD]. It's exactly the same as the Cradle Whip, except that the Lead leads the Follow straight forward on the second (1-2-3) with two hands, letting go, then catches the Follow's shoulders with both hands to send her back along LOD on (4-5-6).

If you get there in time to send the Follow clearly back along LOD on (3), the ending can be a turn with the Follow pivoting back (3), forward (4), back (5), forward (6) along LOD for a **Cradle Whip, Outside Turn** [CWO] or a **Shoulder Whip, Free Spin** [SHF].

Lead's Cradle

In addition to getting the Follow in Cradle, you can also get the Lead in Cradle. Here are two satisfying variations that incorporate Lead's Cradle.

∞

Lead's Cradle Waist Slide [LCW]

From open two-hands, dance a Waist Slide (p. 37), but keep both hands, bringing the right-to-left hands into the frame, passing them over the Leads head. On (4-5-6), use these hands to sweep the Follow across LOD to the outside lane, and retake waltz position.

∞

Lead's Cradle with Pivaloop Free Spin [LCP]

Starts the same as above, but after the right-to-left hands pass over the Lead, bring them down to get the Lead in Cradle for a Waltz Walk on (4-5-6). Then lead a Pivaloop Free Spin (p. 29) for the Follow with the right-to-left hands on (1-2-3-4-5-6). Or stay in Lead's Cradle and lead the Pivaloop Free Spin exit on any subsequent (1).

This could also be a **Lead's Cradle with Pivaloop Double Inside Turn**, or **Lead's Cradle with Pivaloop Rollaway**.

∞

Wrong-Way Cradle

Nothing is actually wrong with this position, the name is just a convenient way of distinguishing it from traditional Cradle. The only real difference between the two positions is which arms are on top. In Cradle, the left-to-right hands are on top, and in Wrong-Way Cradle, the right-to-left hands are on top.

∞

Walkaround Wrap to Wrong-Way Cradle [WRC]

Similar to the Walkaround Wrap to Cradle (p. 120), but after you have open two-hands, on (4-5-6), the Lead turns the Follow CW under the right-to-left arms across LOD in front of him, into Wrong-Way Cradle. She does Orbits footwork to cross LOD.

Behind-the-Back Wrap to Wrong-Way Cradle [BWC]

This was a variation inspired by the Random Dance Move Generator (p. 167), which suggested a "behind-the-back underarm wrap."

(1-2-3) Waist Slide to Lead's Cradle.

(4-5-6) A Follow's CW inside turn with the right-to-left hands into Wrong-Way Cradle. She does Orbits footwork to cross LOD.

The second bar could also be done on any (4-5-6) of a longer Cradle Walk in Lead's Cradle.

∞

Most of the Cradle exits—a single turn or unwind on (4), or double turns starting on (2)—can easily be adapted to exit Wrong-Way Cradle as well.

"Intelligence will take you only so far. Over the long run, how well you relate to others is more important."

— Steven Jarrett

Chapter 24

Empathetic Leading

When we ask Follows what distinguishes their favorite partners, the responses can generally be summed up as, "He actually seems to care about me. It feels like we're dancing together, rather than him just showing off. Everything just works somehow."

Leads, you want to be this "him." But how exactly? In this chapter, we'll share many practical tips for achieving this, starting with one of the most important: leading clearly.

∞

Leading Clearly

"Yare erifepab icimen?"

Dancing with an unclear Lead feels a bit like that. You don't really know what he's saying, but it looks like he's asking a question, so you should probably respond. But how? It's an uncomfortable situation to be in as a Follow.

Leads, your partner is trying to discern, moment by moment, what you're trying to lead and seamlessly translate that into her own movement. In order to do so effectively, she needs a clear lead. Therefore, when leading, it's essential to focus on leading clearly, giving the proper signals at the proper time, i.e., just before she needs to take the corresponding step, so there's no ambiguity that might trip her up.

For example, in a Grapevine, you need to clearly lead each step by rolling your shoulders forward and back. Traveling laterally along LOD, the Follow is wondering which way to cross: alternatively in front and behind, as in a Grapevine, or in front multiple times, as in Cross Swivels (or Waltz Walk). If you don't clearly distinguish between these two possibilities, she could easily trip over her own feet.

There are multiple elements of clear leading.

Leading Decisively

The first element is decisiveness. If you yourself aren't sure what you're leading, there's no way you can provide a clear lead for your partner. Therefore, rather than being wishy-washy, pick something to lead, and lead it! If something unexpected happens, you can (and should) make a mid-course correction, but every choice, from your initial choice of variation to your choice to adapt in the moment, should be made decisively, not second-guessing yourself.

Leading Confidently

The second element of clear leading is confidence. Even once they've chosen something to lead, many Leads are meek in their leading. They're not really sure of themselves, so they lead lightly—too lightly for the Follow to know what they're intending. For the Follow, this is equivalent to trying to interpret a whisper that's too soft to actually be heard. Not only is it impossible to do so, it's annoying to be forced to try.

Actually Leading

The third element is actually leading. Often, in competition ballroom dance, the partners are essentially solo dancers who are dancing corresponding steps in each other's arms. The Lead does his part, and the Follow does hers, but there's little actual leading and following involved.

Some Leads try to apply this same approach to social dancing, i.e., "I give the signal, then she's responsible for her part." The best Leads, however, do not. In addition to signaling the beginning of a variation, they actively help their partner through the whole thing, providing balance, rotation, direction, something to push and pull on, etc. Whatever she needs, they are there to support her through every step of the dance. In other words, they actually lead!

∞

Leading Comfortably

Of course, while you're leading clearly, it's also important to lead comfortably. As we noted in *Waltzing*, "clear leading is the physical equivalent of perfect diction, not shouting." Leading clearly isn't about the amount of force you apply, but how skillfully you apply it.

When it comes to the amount of force, there's an ideal range of not too little and not too much. While this range will vary based on the preferences of the partners and the current dance and variation, you'll generally want to aim somewhere in the middle. On a scale of force from 1 to 10, aim for somewhere between 4 and 7. 1-3 is too wimpy, and 8-10 can be painful.

$$\underbrace{1\ 2\ 3}_{\text{too little}}\ \underbrace{4\ 5\ 6\ 7}_{\text{just right}}\ \underbrace{8\ 9\ 10}_{\text{too much}}$$

Some Leads think that if they err on the side of too light (1-3), they'll be less likely to hurt their partner. But as we saw before, if she doesn't know what he's trying to lead, she's liable to trip and fall. Therefore, it's equally important to avoid both ends of the spectrum, not just the higher end.

Of course, even more important than the amount of force you use is how and when you apply it. For example, when rolling the Follow off your right arm from Cradle Position, you'll want to lead it with your right arm to her back, rather than pulling on her left hand, as the latter will not only be less comfortable but also less clear. In addition, you'll want to wait until (4), when her R is free to step into the CW turn, rather than making her trip over her own feet by trying to turn CW on a forward step with her L.

This is one reason why it's important for Leads to actually read the descriptions (or better yet, take classes), instead of just watching the videos. If you only watch the videos, it's easy to miss the subtle tips like these that are essential for leading comfortably.

∞

Choosing the Right Variations

In addition to considering how you lead each variation, it's important to consider which variations you lead.

While some Leads choose variations on a whim based on what they want to do in the moment, the best Leads choose variations with their partner in mind. There are several important things to consider in this regard:

Difficulty Level

The first consideration when choosing variations is the difficulty level. You want to choose variations that are challenging enough to be interesting for your partner, without being so challenging that it feels like a test. This will vary based on the skill level of your partner.

If you don't already know what your partner's skill level is, it's a good idea to start easy and ramp up from there, rather than throwing them into something more challenging right from the start. For example, when leading, we usually start a dance with some basics and beginning content, e.g., He Goes, She Goes or a Grapevine Outside Turn. Once we see how our partners do with those, we can gauge what to lead next, and continue to adjust from there.

Of course, just because you're dancing with an advanced Follow doesn't mean you should constantly throw her into complicated figures. Even the most experienced Follows appreciate the serene partnering connection that comes with Turning Basics and easygoing figures. And just because you're dancing with a beginning Follow doesn't necessarily mean you should stick only to what she knows. She'll also appreciate you showing her something new, as long as you lead it clearly and comfortably.

Follow's Preferences

Every Follow has figures that she likes more or less than others. As an empathetic Lead, your job is to discern what those are, leading the ones she likes and avoiding the ones she doesn't.

While some Follows will come right out and tell you "I love turns" or "I get really dizzy" (read: "please don't lead a lot of turns"), others will tell you in more subtle ways. Specifically, you can read it from their body language. Watch carefully to see when your partner looks like they're having fun (or not), and adjust the variations you're leading to allow her to have more fun more often.

Of course, you also have your own preferences as a Lead, so the ideal figures will be the ones you both like. But the best Leads put their partner's preferences first.

Floor Space

It's also important to consider how much floor space you have available. For example, you don't want to lead He Goes, Rollaway in the middle of a crowd. This is not only inconsiderate to your partner; it's inconsiderate to everyone around you. Instead, choose safer, more compact variations in traffic, and wait until you have space to dance larger variations.

Musicality

As we noted in Chapter 15, Follows often hear the music better, so they'll appreciate musicality even more than you do as a Lead. Therefore, do your best to follow the guidelines in that chapter to lead the Follow not only comfortably, but musically.

Momentum

Perhaps most importantly, you'll want to consider the Follow's momentum and only lead things that are comfortable from where she currently is.

For example, as we saw in Chapter 10, the Follow alternately turns CW and CCW in a Grapevine. A good Lead considers this, and leads her into the proper turn at the proper time. And in an inside turn from closed position, he waits until (2) to bring the hand through, rather than wrapping it around her neck on (1).

That might sound like a lot of analytical work. To make things easier, instead of analyzing her every step, try focusing on attentive empathy. How will your leading feel from her perspective? With a little practice, your informed instinct will guide you to the specific details we mentioned. In any case, try to ensure that whatever you're leading flows seamlessly from your partner's current momentum, rather than wrenching her out of her reverie.

Putting Connection First

Some Leads feel the need to show off. Whether they're dancing to impress their partner, or their friends who are watching, they prioritize flashy variations and/or non-stop "creativity" that never actually has a satisfying resolution. These Leads are never the most desirable partners. Instead, the best partners are the ones who prioritize connection.

As long as you're truly connecting with your partner, you're both going to have a good time. In fact, some of our favorite dances as Follows have been the ones in which our partners led only a few variations, or maybe even just the Turning Basic for three minutes. No amount of impressive variations can make up for a lack of connection. So don't try to be flashy: put what matters more first—connection.

Avoiding the Washing Machine

If you follow the previous guideline, this one will come naturally, but it's important enough to call out specifically. While many Follows love to turn, no one likes being put through the washing machine. We all know that one Lead who leads a nonstop series of random turns, never giving his partner a chance to breathe. To the untrained eye, he may look impressive, but no one actually likes dancing with him.

Basics are beautiful.

And so are simple, elegantly constructed figures like the ones we've described in this book. Follows much prefer dancing those to being put through the washing machine.

Flexibly Adapting

In every dance you ever have, there will be moments when the Follow does something you don't expect. It's easy to see this as a mistake, by either of you: either she followed it wrong, or you led it wrong. But don't even entertain the thought!

Rather than seeing it as a mistake, by either of you, flexibly adapt to it and see where things go. Welcome chance intrusions into your plan. Don't even let on that anything's wrong (apologizing for yourself, or worse, scolding your partner). It's not wrong, it's simply different from what you expected.

This ability to flexibly adapt to anything, while showing empathy for both your partner and yourself, is one of the essential hallmarks of the best partners, Lead or Follow.

Co-Creating

The best Leads treat their partners as equal co-creators of the dance. Follows aren't puppets, they're dancers. Their own ideas are equally good—sometimes better. Therefore, just as the Follow is looking for ideas from the Lead, the Lead is looking for ideas from the Follow.

This often includes matching the Follow's styling, since she's often the one to lead that part of the dance. But it can also mean looking for opportunities to amplify her choices, just as she amplifies yours. For example, if she's wound up for a turn, lead that turn. Or if she's rotating you more, rotate her more (maybe she's trying to save you from a crash!). In moments like these, it's almost like you're deciding on the next step together (maybe you are).

Having Fun

The easiest way to be a popular partner is simply to have fun while dancing! Follows of all experience levels tell us that even if a Lead isn't the best dancer, as long as he's having fun, he's fun to dance with. So have fun, and let it show, and both of you will find even greater enjoyment on the dance floor.

We've given you a lot to think about in this chapter, beyond all the other things you were already thinking about. But if you can, stop overthinking the details and just focus on having a good time with your partner. If you're succeeding at that, that's what ultimately matters. Everything else is simply a way to help you get there!

Chapter 25

Shadow Position Variations

This family of easy waltz figures can be done walking forward along LOD instead of constantly rotating. Some figures have Country-Western origins, some vernacular and folk, and some come from round dancing. One advantage of knowing these figures is to be able to dance with people who don't know how to do a rotating waltz, for instance, dancing with a non-dancing friend at a wedding, who will be thrilled that they're waltzing.

∞

Shadow Position

In Shadow Position, the Follow is at the side of the Lead, with both dancers holding their hands comfortably near the Follow's shoulders, a bit above shoulder height, with arms in a "W" position, left hand in left hand, and right hand in right hand. The Follow can be at either the Lead's right side or left side but doesn't like it when the Lead is directly behind her back.

The default footwork for Shadow Position variations, unless otherwise specified, is a simple Waltz Walk, traveling along LOD.

Leads: Keep your hands slightly front of the Follow, rather than pulling them back behind her.

Follows: To feel more connected to your partner in Shadow Position, gently brace forward into his hands. This will also help keep the hands in front of you.

Shadow Position was called Varsovienne Position a century ago, and is sometimes called Cape or Horseshoe Position today. Sweetheart is also a popular name for it, but that name is sometimes applied to Cradle and Skater's Positions as well, leading to confusion. We prefer the term Shadow because it's more specific.

Entrances to Shadow Position

Grapevine Outside Turn to Shadow [GTS]

A Grapevine Outside Turn as you know it (p. 44), but changing hands on the turn like so:

(4-5-6) As the Follow turns under the Lead's left arm, he transfers her right hand into his right hand, directly over her head, then catches her free left hand in his left hand as she's facing forward, to take Shadow Position. The Follow turns a bit more to end up facing along LOD, rather than facing the Lead.

Creative Note: This maneuver can also be done during any other outside turn for the Follow on the outside lane. Or if you're already holding right-in-right for a CW turn in the outside lane, simply catch the Follow when she's facing forward by offering left-to-left to stabilize her. Or if she's turning CW under right-to-left hands, simply pass her left hand into his left when she's facing forward, then take right-in-right.

Inside Flip to Shadow [IFS]

This quick and efficient entrance to Shadow Position was created by Woodley Packard.

(1) A non-rotating cross-step along LOD.

(2-3) The Lead turns the Follow CCW as in an inside turn, but places her right hand into his right at shoulder level.

(4-5-6) Once she's facing forward again, he takes her left hand in Shadow Position.

The Follow stays in the outside lane the whole time, and the Lead on the inside lane.

He Goes to Shadow [HSH]

(1-2-3) He Goes (p. 33), passing under his left arm and in front of her to the outside lane.

(4-5-6) As in a Lead's Underarm Turn (p. 36), the Lead immediately sweeps the Follow across LOD as she crosses in front of him to the outside lane, rotating one full turn CW. As she passes in front of him, the Lead places her right hand into his right, passing that arm over her head, then takes her left hand in his left in Shadow Position.

Creative Note: The second bar of this transition can also be done in place of any other Follow's sweep across LOD on (4-5-6).

He Goes, She Goes to Shadow [HSS]

(1-6) The first two bars of He Goes, She Goes (p. 33).

(1-2-3) The third bar of He Goes, She Goes, i.e., the inside turn, but as the Follow finishes the turn, the Lead catches her right hand in his right, taking her left hand in Shadow Position with a steadying lead. During the turn, the Lead can sneak behind her to the inside lane, to end up in Shadow Position with the Follow at his right.

(4-5-6) Continue walking forward in Shadow Position.

∞

Waist Slide to Shadow [WSS]

Dance a Waist Slide (p. 37), but after the Lead's left hand breaks free, he offers it to her as she's flying by his left side. His left arm acts like a flipper, with his left elbow remaining where it is, at his lower left ribcage, and his left forearm flipping open, to offer his left hand.

She takes his left hand with her free left hand and flips CW across LOD in front of him with Orbits footwork on (4-5-6) to face along LOD in the outside lane. There, he takes her right hand in his right, in Shadow Position.

∞

Peeling Off to Shadow [PLS]

This is the Shadow Position equivalent of the Walkaround Wrap to Cradle (p. 120).

During the first half a Turning Basic, the Lead peels off to the outside lane, disengaging his right hand from the Follow's shoulder and placing it into her right hand, then walks CW behind her to take her left in his left when he gets to the inside lane.

Leads: While you're moving around her, clearly lead her to continue walking straight forward along LOD the whole time.

∞

R-in-R Wrap to Shadow [WTS]

If you turn the Follow under right-in-right hands, and bring the hands down after the turn, the right hands will be wrapped in front of the Follow, a popular position in Country Two Step, known as The Wrap. From The Wrap, you can simply lead an Inside Flip to Shadow with the right-in-right hands.

For example, dance a Swingout Tuck Turn (p. 89), changing to right-in-right hands for the tuck before the CW turn on (4-5-6), ending up in The Wrap on (1). Then turn the Follow CCW on (2-3) into Shadow Position.

Variations in Shadow Position

Shadow Walk [SWK]

Simply walk forward in Shadow Position. The default is to have the Follow at the right side.

∞

Side Slips to Change Sides [SSC]

While walking, you can change sides with your partner. The Follow passes in front of the Lead from his right to his left, or vice versa, as the Lead passes behind her, crossing trails.

Note: Some Leads simply pass the Follow back and forth in front of him without moving himself, but Follows prefer it when he moves as well.

∞

Shadow Wheel [SWH]

In Shadow Position with the Follow at the Lead's right, lead the Follow forward as the Lead backs up, turning CCW as a couple. A full turn is customarily done in two bars of music, but watch your partner, rotating them comfortably, instead of forcing it to happen in two bars.

This variation is most comfortable when it turns on the spot, rather than rolling along LOD.

If the Follow happens to be at his left side, she travels forward CW around him. Either way, the Follow continues her forward momentum in this version.

Although leading the Follow forward is traditional, it's not illegal for the Lead to travel forward around the Follow. In this case, the Lead makes sure to gently rotate himself forward around the Follow instead of pulling her backward with force. This also rotates the other direction if the Follow is at his left side.

∞

Shadow Underarm Turn [SUT]

The Lead raises the left hands, and circles them forward around in front of the Follow, to turn her once CW, keeping her at his right side. The right hands are released, then retaken in Shadow Position when she's facing forward again.

Or the Lead can turn the Follow under the right hands, releasing and retaking the left hands. Both options are shown in the video.

In either case, this is most comfortable and musical when led on (4). She pivots forward R (4), back L (5), forward R (6). It can also be done any time she's on her R, i.e., (2) or (6) work too. But it doesn't work when she's on her L, i.e., (1), (3), or (5).

Rather than thinking about the counts, it's often better to just watch her footwork in your peripheral vision, and lead it when she's about to step onto her R.

Shadow Underarm Turn to Lead's Shadow [STL]

In addition to the Follow being in front in Shadow Position, the Lead can also be in front. Here's an easy transition from Follow at Lead's right to Lead at Follow's right.

Start a Shadow Underarm Turn, but keep both hands, using them to lead the Follow behind his back into the inside lane. She pivots CW on her R to face against LOD, then walks forward behind his back from his right side to his left (a half circle CW).

Now the right hands are at his right shoulder, and the left hands are at his left shoulder, with the Follow's right arm behind his shoulders.

Follow's Flip in Front to Shadow [FFF]

From Lead's Shadow, the Lead uses both hands to turn the Follow CW across in front of him.

The optimal footwork is the same as the Follow's half of Orbits, flipping across LOD in three steps, starting Follow's right, i.e., on an even count, most commonly (4).

Leads: Again, use your peripheral vision to determine when her R is free for this.

Mixmaster [MIX]

Dance the Shadow Underarm Turn to Lead's Shadow and Follow's Flip in Front to Shadow one right after the other, perhaps several times in a row.

It works best for her if each half of the variation is initiated on (4), i.e., her R.

Mixmaster (Superspeed Version) [MXS]

If you're careful about it, Mixmaster can be danced in a short six counts.

The first half starts on (4), and the second half starts on (2).

See the video for the exact footwork, although we don't recommend you think about that. Instead, Leads, strongly dos-a-dos CW around your partner as you lead the first half on (4) and the second half on (2). The second half leads directly into the next first half, with the Follow continuously pivoting (2-3-4) without stopping.

Important Note: If you don't make it, don't force it. If she's not in position by (2) or (4), delay the lead to another even count.

∞

Multiple Shadow Underarm Turns [MSU]

Same as the basic Shadow Underarm Turn, keeping the Follow on the outside lane, but the Follow turns more than once under the raised arms.

The same notes that apply to a single Shadow Underarm Turn apply to multiple turns as well, i.e., you can lead them with either hand, but in either case, you need to start them when she's stepping on her R—on (2), (4), or (6).

∞

Shadow Splits [SHS]

Same as The Splits (p. 20), but in Shadow Position.

Separate from your partner, going diagonally forward to the inside and outside respectively, then travel forward diagonally toward each other to meet again. (As you travel forward, your paths will form a diamond shape.) Give your partner a reassuring look, to let them know you're not abandoning them.

This is useful for passing around an obstacle, like a couple stopping with a Shadow Wheel right in front of you, or playfully leap-frogging another unsuspecting couple.

∞

Lead's Foot Fudge to Parallel Feet

Several particularly satisfying Shadow variations require parallel feet, i.e., the Lead and Follow stepping on the same foot at the same time.

To get into parallel feet, the lead changes his feet ("foot fudges"), to step L when the Follow is stepping L (or R when she's stepping R). To do this, take 2 steps to 3 counts of music. You can do this at any time, but try to do it as quietly as possible, so she doesn't think she should change her feet too. (Taking 4 steps in 3 counts is also possible, but usually more noticeable.)

We could have specified a particular method and timing for making this change, but we've found that this specification isn't practical, because it's not remembered weeks later. It's more effective to simply know that the Lead must foot-fudge to match his partner's feet.

Try switching your feet, then check, with your peripheral vision, to make sure you succeeded.

∞

The Windmill [WIN]

This figure is famous. It's done in Shadow Position with parallel footwork. Wait until the second bar of music, on (4), when both R feet are free.

Here are the feet:

Both step forward R (1), side L (2), back R (3), back L (4), side R (5), and forward L (6). Both stay in your own lane the whole time, Lead on the inside and Follow on the outside.

And here are the arms:

Keep the arms extended and angled up and down throughout, in graceful imitation of a windmill (or two parallel windmills).

As you both rotate CW, bring the left hands up and the right hands down on the first half, then vice versa on the second half. When the left hands reach the back of her head, pass them high over her head, and when the right hands reach the front of his torso, break through, as in a Waist Slide, retaking those hands behind his back. Similarly, when the right hands reach the front of her head, pass them high over her head, and when the left hands reach his back, break through, retaking those hands in front of his torso.

The video will make all of this much clearer.

∞

Illusion Turn [ILT]

This is also done with parallel footwork, starting with the R feet on the second bar.

Starting in Shadow Position with the Follow at the right, both pivot forward R (4), back L (5), forward R (6), keeping the Follow in front of the Lead the whole time. During these steps, the Lead passes behind the Follow while they're both showing their backs along LOD. You end up in Shadow Position with the Follow at the left.

If you slip the Follow across in front from left to right on (1-2-3), you can immediately repeat it on the next (4-5-6).

∞

Shadow Waltz [SHW]

This is also done with parallel footwork, starting with the R feet on the second bar.

Locking in to a strong, close Shadow Position with the Follow at the right, both dance the Waterfall step (p. 16), side-by-side, rotating CW as a couple you travel along LOD.

∞

To get out of parallel feet, simply do a Lead's foot fudge again.

∞

Skater's and Hammerlock Positions

Traditional Skater's Position in waltzing is more than two centuries old, illustrated in *A Description of the Correct Method of Waltzing* by Thomas Wilson, London, 1816. The Follow is at the right side of the Lead, with right-in-right hands comfortably at her right waist, and left-in-left hands held in front of the Lead. But the Follow can also be at the Lead's left side, their left hands at her left waist.

Hammerlock Position is similar, but the hand at the waist is now behind the back. As a wrestling move, Hammerlock is supposed to hurt, when the hand is forced up behind the victim's back. Therefore, to be comfortable, always keep this hand low, just above the tailbone, especially when transitioning.

In general, Skater's is the preferred position for the Follow, since it's more comfortable for her and avoids any danger associated with the hand behind the back. Conversely, Hammerlock is the preferred position for the Lead. This is also because it's more comfortable for the Follow, given that the hand she's holding behind his back is closer to her than it would be if it was at his far waist.

∞

The next six variations based on Skater's and Hammerlock were created by Peggy Leiby and Ret Turner from Mostly Waltz in Philadelphia.

Lasso Transition from Shadow Position to Left Hammerlock [LAS]

From Shadow with the Follow at the right side, the Lead raises the left hands and circles them out over the Follow's head, as he lowers the right hands (don't let go), and she turns CW to face back against LOD.

With the raised left hands, he leads her behind his back to the inside lane, with a motion like a lasso, around to his left side. His right hand is placed in Hammerlock Position behind his back, and his left hand is in front of her.

As usual, initiate this on (4), or another count when her R is free to turn CW.

∞

Flip Transition from Left Hammerlock to Left Skater's [FHS]

The Follow is at the Lead's left side, and remains at his left side throughout this transition.

The Lead releases his right hands and brings the left hands back in between them, to turn the Follow CW, immediately lowering that hand behind her back to her left waist. He offers his right hand in front and she takes it with her right.

This is also a CW turn for the Follow, so it should be led on an even count, maybe the next (4).

∞

Inside Turn Transition from Left Hammerlock to Left Skater's [IHS]

Starts and ends the same as above, but has an extra inside turn in the middle.

After bringing the left hands through, the Lead circles her head with a high hand for a CW inside turn, lowering her hand at the end of her second rotation, behind her back, to her left waist. End in the same Left Skater's Position as above.

∞

Lasso Transition from Left Skater's to Right Hammerlock [LSH]

From Skater's with the Follow at the Lead's left, the Lead raises the right hands and circles them out over the Follow's head to turn her CCW, then, with a lasso motion, leads her to walk forward behind his back, to his right side. His left hand remains low the entire time, and ends behind his back in Hammerlock Position.

This is a CCW turn, so it's only comfortable when the Follow is stepping onto her L, on (1), or another odd count.

Flip Transition from Right Hammerlock to Right Skater's [FRH]

The Follow is at the Lead's right side, and remains at his right side throughout this transition.

The Lead releases his left hands and brings the right hands back in between them, to turn the Follow CCW, immediately lowering that hand behind her back to her right waist. He offers his left hand in front, and she takes it.

This is also a CCW turn, so it should also be led on an odd count, maybe the next (1).

∞

Inside Turn Transition from Right Hammerlock to Right Skater's [IHR]

Starts and ends the same as above, but has an extra inside turn in the middle.

After bringing the right hands through, the Lead circles her head with a high hand for a CCW inside turn, lowering her hand at the end of her second rotation, behind her back, to her right waist. End in the same Right Skater's Position as above.

∞

Exits from Shadow Position

Face Loop from Shadow Position [FLS]

(1-2-3) Just walk in Shadow Position with the Follow at the Lead's right.

(4-5-6) Start a Shadow Underarm Turn with left-in-left hands, but after the left hands loop the Follow's head, they also loop his head, "combing his right ear," and her left drops onto his right shoulder. He lets go of right hands as she's turning, then catches her in waltz position with both hands after the face loop.

∞

In this and all other transitions, if the Lead previously foot-fudged to do Windmill, Illusion Turns, or Shadow Waltz, and hasn't yet foot-fudged out, he'll need to do so now to get his R free for the primary cross-step on (1).

∞

Face Loop from Skater's Position [FLK]

The same, but as an exit from Right Skater's Position.

Free Spin from Shadow Position [FFS]

(1-2-3) Just walk in Shadow Position with the Follow at the Lead's right.

(4-5-6) With both hands, lead a CW Follow's free spin. She turns 3/4 to her right, to face him, and they take closed position.

Some dancers prefer to keep the right-in-right hands throughout, passing her right hand into his left, which makes this more of a flip than a free spin.

∞

Sombrero from Shadow Position [SFS]

(1) Just walk in Shadow Position. Her R isn't free yet.

(2-3) The Lead turns the Follow CW under the left hands, while keeping the right hands.

(4-5-6) With a continuing motion, he loops his right hand up in front of her face and down behind the back of her head, while at the same time looping his own head in the same way with his left hand.

Try something from this new Sombrero position. Perhaps a Traveling Swingout to catch swingout hands, or maybe a Neck Roll Dip (p. 154) or transition to Role Reversal (p. 174).

∞

Zillertaler Arms

This position of the arms, borrowed from the Zillertaler Ländler, an Austrian folk dance, is a puzzle, but you'll feel quite accomplished when you successfully get into them.

∞

Double Turn to Zillertaler Arms [ZIL]

From Shadow with the Follow at the Lead's right, initiate a double turn for the Follow on (2). She continues to turn under (3-4-5-6). Keep holding both hands above the Follow's head the whole time, then bring the left hands down between you at the end.

You should end up with the left-in-left hands resting at the bottom of a triangular window formed by the right arms. The right-in-right hands point straight up. See your partner through the window.

Recommence waltzing while holding Zillertaler Arms. The most comfortable footwork for the Follow is often Co-Waterfall (p. 47).

∞

Face Loop Exit from Zillertaler Arms [FZL]

To get out of Zillertaler Arms, keep waltzing while leading a face loop with the left-in-left hands on (4-5-6), letting go of the right-in-right hands and taking waltz position for a regular Turning Basic.

∞

Pop Turns

These turns, borrowed from Country Two Step, are an efficient way to transition between Shadow, Cradle, and Skater's Positions.

∞

Pop Turn from Shadow to Cradle [PSC]

(1) From Shadow with the Follow at the Lead's right, use both hands to rotate the Follow very slightly CW (away from the Lead) in preparation for a CCW turn on (2).

(2-3) Using the left hands, turn the Follow CCW, as she steps back R, forward L. As she turns, the Lead brings the left hands down between them and passes it into his right hand at waist level. Then take left-to-right hands in front in Cradle Position.

∞

Pop Turn from Cradle to Shadow [PCS]

(1) From Cradle, use both hands to rotate the Follow very slightly CW (away from the Lead) in preparation for a CCW turn on (2).

(2-3) Using the left hands, turn the Follow CCW, as she steps back R, forward L. As she turns, the Lead brings the left hands between them and passes it into his right hand at shoulder level. Then take left hands in front in Shadow Position.

Pop Turn from Cradle to Skater's [PCK]

Same as the Pop Turn from Cradle to Shadow, except the Lead passes her right hand into his right hand at waist level to end up in Skater's Position.

Pop Turn from Skater's to Cradle [PKC]

Aside from a slightly different starting position, it's exactly the same as the Pop Turn from Shadow to Cradle.

In addition to transitioning between positions, the Pop Turn framework allows for fancy double turns in Shadow and Cradle.

Double Pop Turn in Shadow [DPS]

(1) From Shadow with the Follow at the Lead's right, use both hands to rotate the Follow very slightly CW (away from the Lead) in preparation for a CCW turn on (2).

(2-3) Using the left hands, turn the Follow CCW, as she steps back R, forward L. Unlike the transition to Cradle, keep the hands high, passing over the Follow's head, an outside turn.

(4-5) Taking the right hands, and dropping the left hands, continue turning the Follow CCW as she keeps pivoting, back R, forward L. This second turn under right-in-right is an inside turn.

(6) Retaking left hands, stabilize in Shadow Position and recommence walking forward.

You can also do a **Single Pop Turn in Shadow** [SPS], which is just the first half of this figure, catching in Shadow again the first time the Follow is facing forward.

Double Pop Turn in Cradle [DPC]

Same as the Double Pop Turn in Shadow, but with different, somewhat trickier, hands.

The first turn is an inside turn for the Follow under the left-to-right hands. The second turn feels like the Follow is tunneling under the right-to-left hands. The video will clarify exactly how this works.

Leads: This isn't something to lead on an unsuspecting Follow. First, lead some basic pop turns to practice the basic dynamic, then lead the Shadow Double to practice the dynamic of the double. Only consider leading the Cradle Double when you know that everything it's based on is already working comfortably.

Follows: In this and all of the other pop turns, keep your hands where they are, rather than trying to anticipate where they should be. If you move them in anticipation of what's to come, the Lead won't be able to find them.

You can also do a **Single Pop Turn in Cradle** [SPC], which is just the first half of this figure. It's an inside turn with the left-to-right hands, the hands behind her back briefly disconnecting to allow the Follow to break through them before taking Cradle position again.

Chapter 26

Putting the Social in Social Dance

An essay by UT student Zach Kosut.

∞

Over the past semester, I've realized that my ability to execute moves had little to do with my sense of enjoyment in comparison to the connection between my partner and I. I had dances where I pulled out every move in my pocket and my partner followed flawlessly, yet a lack of enthusiasm and a focus on technique made the dance feel mechanical; a coordinated series of movements as charming as a group of people exiting an elevator.

However, an approach that emphasizes the "social" in "social dance" changes the experience. A dance becomes a shared experience, a communion. Like jamming with other musicians or cooking with a friend, the final product does not characterize the experience as much as the community present.

The more I concentrated on my partner and finding that connection, the more enjoyment I took away from the class. In some dances, it was obvious that both partners wanted to whirl for two minutes straight; other times we were both content to stick with the basic steps and keep the rhythm while making conversation.

Once I began to evaluate my dancing in terms of my ability to read my partner rather than how many moves I employed, I became much more pleased with myself and confident in my ability to have a good time on a dance floor. The idea that the priority in the arts is not perfection, but fulfillment, changes the way I look at my favorite pastimes.

"Dance to express,
not to impress."

— Anonymous

Chapter 27

Ways to Conclude a Waltz with Flair

In Chapter 15, we talked about using your dancing to punctuate the music. A particularly good place to do this is the end of the song. Therefore, in this chapter, you'll learn a variety of different ways to conclude a waltz with flair.

Note on Timing: In an ideal world, the Lead would know that the song was ending, and would lead one of these concluding figures at exactly the right time. But in the real world of freestyle social dancing, that rarely happens. Instead, Leads, aim to hit the end of the song, but don't worry if you lead it a little early, or a little late. The fact that you made the effort to bring the dance to a satisfying close matters much more than your exact timing.

Turns

One of the most common ways to end a waltz is simply to lead one final flourish.

∞

Ending with a Turn [EWT]

Lead any Follow's underarm turn variation (e.g., a Grapevine Outside Turn), then simply stop and face your partner at the end of the turn.

You can then "honor partners" with a bow/curtsy, or simply stand tall.

∞

Ending with a Genuflection [GEN]

Same as above, but the Lead genuflects, i.e., drops down to one knee at the end.

Dips

Another elegant way to end a waltz is with a dip. While the basic idea is always the same, there are many different dip stylings.

∞

Tips for Dips

Follows: For all of the dips in this section, you'll step side R, putting your weight on it, then turn 90° CCW to face toward your L, which is extended, toe to the floor. Then lean back, forming a straight line from the top of your head to the tip of your left toes. For a safe dip, lean back only as far as you can support your own weight on your R, rather than throwing yourself into it and relying on him to support you. (He *will* support you, but it's good to be extra safe!) As you lean back, don't throw your head back ("showing your neck to the guillotine"), or crunch your head forward (which communicates that you don't trust him). Finally, and most importantly, don't dip yourself unless you're sure that's what he's leading.

Leads: You'll step side L, taking a solid, stable stance, as you rotate the Follow's body 90° CCW, keeping your partner straight in front of you, her right hip lined up with your center. You don't rotate at all. That last point is particularly important: Melissa had to have knee surgery because a Lead rotated himself while dipping her! Never send the Follow around your left side, as in a cross-body inside turn to the inside lane. Always keep her straight in front of you, rotating her 90° CCW on the spot. Although some Follows will support themselves, others may not. In either case, it's your responsibility to support her. If you're not confident in supporting her, don't lead the dip!

Both: For the handhold, we generally recommend Barrel Hold, with both of the Lead's arms under both of the Follow's, both of his hands behind her shoulders. To get there, the Lead can toss her right hand from his left hand onto his left shoulder as he leads into the dip. Where do you look in a dip? It's entirely up to you. Both can look out (at "the audience"), both can look at each other ("how romantic!"), or one can look at the other while the other looks out.

∞

Tango Dip [DIP]

(1) A non-rotating cross-step along LOD.

(2) Dip side along LOD, and hold.

This can also be done out of any cross in front for the Follow, for example, the Follow's cross in front on (5) of a Grapevine or any primary cross-step in a Follow's Solo.

Hesitating Tango Dip [HTD]

The above dip can also be done as a hesitation the middle of a dance, like so:

(1) Primary cross-step.

(2-3) Dip side along LOD (2), and hold (3).

(4-5) Bring the Follow back up to standing, both shifting weight to the rear foot.

(6) Take weight on the forward foot, ready to re-commence with the primary cross-step.

∞

Inside Turn Dip [ITD]

Similar to the Tango Dip, but with an inside turn first.

Cross (1), CCW inside turn, Follow pivoting back, forward (2-3), then catch for the dip along LOD on (4), and hold.

∞

Face Loop Dip [FLD]

Going into a dip on (2), the left-to-right hands can pass through the frame and loop in front of her face (without leading any additional rotation), coming to rest on her left shoulder. Once the hands loop her face, let go: while the loop itself is pretty and elegant, holding the final looped position can feel a bit like a chokehold.

This can also be done after an inside turn, for an **Inside Turn Face Loop Dip** [IFD] on (4).

∞

Toss Across Dip [TOD]

Going into a dip on (2) or (4), the Lead can toss the Follow across from his right side to his left side, catching her back with his left arm, and sliding his right hand down her left arm into mirrored waltz position. It's particularly nice when both elegantly look and point the hands back toward the trailing feet.

Free Spin Dip [FSD]

Get right-to-left hands, perhaps from a Hand-to-Hand Zig-Zag (p. 89) or Cradle Yo Yo (p. 124).

Then lead into a Follow's CCW free spin on (2-3), catching your partner for a dip on (4).

The orientation of the free spin can either be along LOD, if the Lead is ahead of her, or into the center, if they're side by side facing along LOD. Whichever one it is, the Lead should clearly lead the free spin in the intended direction, rather than just spinning her randomly.

Follows: The footwork is the same as the Inside Turn Dip. Just be sure to travel straight with your solo pivot steps, rather than veering toward him or away from him.

Leads: After you release her for the free spin, watch for her back, catching it with your right hand and continuing to rotate her into the dip.

∞

Sombrero Neck Roll Dip [SND]

This one isn't everyone's cup of tea, but if the Follow likes neck rolls, it's great fun.

From Shadow Position, dance Sombrero from Shadow Position (p. 145). From Sombrero position, lead a CCW turn under the right arm which is over her shoulders, a neck roll (see hints below). As in the Inside Turn Dip, she pivots back, forward along LOD (2-3), and steps side into a dip on (4).

Leads: To lead a neck roll, rotate her CCW with your right hand on her shoulders as you raise your right elbow just enough to pass it over her head. Keep your right hand on her shoulders the whole time to stabilize her.

Follows: Bend your neck forward to pass your head and neck under his right arm, while focusing on pivoting straight down LOD, staying close to him. If you veer away from him, he won't be able to help support you.

Important Note: Some Follows *hate* neck rolls. Leads, this move is best led with someone who you already know likes neck rolls, particularly since this will be her final impression of you!

∞

Valentino Dip [VTD]

This one is from 1970s disco dancing. From Shadow Position, a CW half turn for the Follow on (4-5-6) into Windows position, with the left-in-left hands over right-in-right. On (1-2-3), use the right hands to bring the Follow back CCW under the left hands, then keep her turning a quarter turn CCW more with the left hands into a dip on (4) with left-in-left held over her head, catching each other's left shoulders or waists with your right hands. The left-in-left hands should form a pretty curve, framing her.

Side Dips

Side dips are another category of dips in which the partners are next to each other, with the Follow leaning sideways, supported by the Lead's side.

Tips for Side Dips

Before leading a side dip, your sides must actually be touching, and you must be exactly side by side, not in front of or behind each other, otherwise: (a) she'll crash forcefully into him, or (b) she'll slide off his side to the front or back.

When leaning, both bodies should be straight from head to toe, and stiff as a board, rather than bending over at the waist.

Cradle Side Dip [CSD]

From Cradle Position, dance Cradle Yo Yo (p. 124), then catch in a strong, close Cradle Position with her left side touching his right. The Lead then steps side L, leaning slightly to the left, as the Follow leans slightly left onto his right side, sharing weight.

This can also be led into by dancing only the second half of Cradle Yo Yo if you're already holding right-to-left hands.

Follows: You can leave your R down next to your L, slide it up your left leg somewhat (a pretty styling), or you can cross it in front of your left, which is not only safe, but a popular style for this dip in Blues/Fusion.

Face-to-Face Side Dip [FFD]

In this version of the side dip, the partners are facing opposite directions, with her right side touching his right side.

Dance half of a Turning Basic (1-2-3), then stop the Follow at the Lead's right side (4-5-6), Lead facing in, Follow facing out, right sides touching. His left side is pointed against LOD, and her left side is pointed along LOD. Then lead into a side dip to the Lead's left (Follow's right) on (1).

Lunges

Borrowed from Tango, lunges are another dramatic way to end a waltz. Leads, in any lunge, remember to gently "land the plane," rather than dragging her to the floor.

Tango Lunge and Close [TLC]

Dance the Hesitating Tango Lunge (p. 62), but make a dramatic slide against LOD on (4), then draw the forward foot closed.

∞

Left Turn with Tango Close [LTC]

This one isn't a lunge, but it's closely related to the previous figure.

Cross (1), then back the Follow across LOD to the inside lane with an easy-going half pivot step (2), and dramatically slide side along LOD, toward the elbows side (3), then draw the free foot closed.

If the Lead backs across LOD on (2) instead, it's a **Right Turn with Tango Close** [RTC].

∞

Inside Turn to Cradle Lunge [ICE]

Dance the Inside Turn to Cradle Lunge (p. 124), but hold the lunge on (4).

Note that this lunge is onto outside feet, not inside feet like the first figure.

∞

Reverse Pivot to Follow's Lunge [RPE]

Dance the Reverse Pivot to Follow's Lunge (p. 108), holding the lunge on (4).

In this one, the Follow is lunging forward R along LOD, straight into the Lead.

∞

Follow's Solo Corte [FSE]

Dance the Follow's Solo Corte (p. 60), holding the lunge on (4).

This one also has the Follow is lunging forward R into the Lead, but this time she's facing against LOD.

Chapter 28

The Beauty in the Good Enough

An essay by Stanford student Mengyi Xu.

∞

I have been trained to always strive for perfection, no matter how painful the process is, and no matter how trivial the end result turns out to be. But most often, perfection is not the most Pareto-efficient outcome. Good enough is.

Social dance freed me from the rigid conception of how something ought to be. Thereby, I have been able to better enjoy the journey. Social dance values alternative interpretations, and enables individuality within a broad framework. Letting go of perfection has allowed me to experiment with different versions of good enough. That flexibility in turn has enabled me to learn from each iteration, and discover something perfect in each good-enough movement.

When I let go of perfection, I become a better version of myself. I am no longer fixated on the intangible ideal. Instead, I calibrate my weaknesses and strengths to the reality that is the moment. My realization of each movement becomes a contextualized response to the music, to my partner's lead, and to the dynamic environment as I experience it. When I let go of perfection, I let go of the burden to perform to a pre-defined standard. My partner and my coordinated execution becomes the benchmark against which a particular movement is measured.

When I let go of perfection, I am no longer searching. I begin to create. I am no longer pigeon-holed into a particular vision. I begin to see my horizons broaden as one good-enough movement follows another. Perfection is a lonely endeavor, but good enough is rewardingly collaborative. Social dance has taught me to see the beauty in the good enough.

"Nobody cares if you can't dance well.
Just get up and dance.
Great dancers are not great because of their technique,
they are great because of their passion."

— Martha Graham

Chapter 29

The Cross-Step Waltz Mixer and Variations

Waltz mixers are especially sociable, allowing you to briefly dance with dozens of partners within a few minutes. There are many Rotary Waltz mixers, but this is the quintessential mixer for Cross-Step Waltz, popular around the world.

∞

The Cross-Step Waltz Mixer [CWM]

(Four Bars) With couples arranged in a large circle with even spacing, all do two Turning Basics traveling along LOD, ending by opening up to face into the center with the Follow on the right, all taking hands in a circle. Leads, note that you stay facing into the center of the circle after one and a half rotations, rather than completing two full turns like the Follow does. If there are too many couples to fit in one circle, two or three concentric circles may be needed.

(Two Bars) All step forward one step, then close in place two steps. Step back one step, then close in place two steps. A social convention is to look at your next partner as you step forward, then look at your current partner as you step back. If the circle is getting too small or too big, the size of these steps can be adjusted to help reshape the circle.

(Two Bars) The Lead turns the next Follow (the one to his left) CCW under his left arm with an inside turn as he does half of a non-turning basic (cross-open-open, R-L-R) behind her into her place, and she does half of a non-turning basic (cross-open-open, L-R-L) passing in front of him into his place, turning under his arm. Then, facing along LOD, the Lead sweeps the Follow into the outside lane into his right arm as she steps forward R toward the outside lane (4), steps side L toward the outside (5), and pulls her right shoulder back (6). You end up in waltz position with the hands pointing along LOD to recommence from the beginning.

Note: If there are extra, unpaired dancers who want to participate, they can place themselves between couples and walk along as everyone dances. When the circle forms, they'll get a partner. The dancer whose next partner was just stolen then does the same.

Cross-Step Waltz Mixer Variations

The Cross-Step Waltz Mixer traditionally begins with two Turning Basics, but these can also be replaced with variations.

Doing variations during the first four bars of the mixer presents a unique challenge. The variations must travel uniformly along LOD to keep up with the other couples. Then, instead of finishing a variation in closed position with the Lead facing out as usual, you must finish side-by-side facing in, with the Lead's right hand holding the Follow's left. You have very little time to adapt to your new partner's frame and style, so the Lead must instantly ascertain how experienced his new partner is, if he wishes to lead something tricky. And both partners must be careful about exiting smoothly, without crashing into the next person.

The majority of Cross-Step Waltz variations don't work in the mixer. Some don't travel consistently along LOD. Others don't resolve within four bars. And others don't flow smoothly from waltz position to the circle. But here are a few that work especially well.

∞

Turning Basic and Grapevine Inside Turn [MGI]

A Turning Basic, then slip out to two hands for a Two-Hand Grapevine Inside Turn (p. 45), in which the Follow turns under the rear (i.e., right-to-left) hands.

The beauty of this sequence is that you still get to enjoy a Turning Basic with your partner, and then, after the variation, you already have the hands you need for the circle.

If you want to do a longer grapevine, you can replace the Turning Basic with six counts of grapevine, and dance a **Six-Count Grapevine, Outside Turn and Free Spin** [MSG], taking right-to-left hands to face in after the free spin.

Or you could do **Chained Grapevine Turns** [MCG]. Start with a three-count grapevine and turn (of any kind), then do another three-count grapevine and turn. The Grapevine Inside Turn is the smoothest choice for the second turn, as it leaves you with the requisite hands.

∞

Turning Basic and Waist Slide [MWS]

A Turning Basic, then a Waist Slide (p. 37). As the Follow flies by his left side, he takes her free left hand in his right to face into the circle.

The beauty of the Waist Slide is that you get to see each other at the end as he starts to face into the center and she flies by in front of him.

Cross-Body Inside Turn to Pivaloop Free Spin [MCP]

This one is good for Follows who like to turn. Lead straight into a Cross-Body Inside Turn to Pivaloop Free Spin (p. 29), taking right-to-left hands to face in after the free spin.

Although you don't get to dance a Turning Basic with your partner, it's a particularly satisfying four-bar figure with a natural transition into the circle.

∞

Halo Frisbee [MHF]

This is another satisfying four-bar figure for Follows who like to turn. Lead straight into Halo Frisbee (p. 28), taking right-to-left hands to face in after the second free spin.

∞

Walkaround Wrap to Cradle, Roll-Off-the-Arm [MWR]

A Walkaround Wrap to Cradle (p. 120) for two bars. Waltz Walk in Cradle for three steps, releasing the hands held in front on (3). Then the Follow rolls off his arm on (4-5-6), ending facing in, holding the hand that you need for the circle.

∞

Walkaround Wrap to Cradle with Outside and Inside Turn Exit [MWD]

Here's a fancier version of that. A Walkaround Wrap to Cradle, then an Outside and Inside Turn Exit from Cradle (p. 122), in which the Follow turns once under the left-to-right hands, and then again under the right-to-left hands, which are what you need for the circle.

Remember to wait until (2) to lead the double turn exit when her outside foot is free to turn CW. If you don't make it to Cradle in time to comfortably unwind her on (2), just wait to Roll-Off-the-Arm on (4), as above.

This one is fun because it starts off like a Turning Basic, but also includes Cradle Position, an Outside Turn, and an Inside Turn, all in four short bars.

If both turns are led with the right-to-left hands (an unwind followed by an inside turn), it's a **Walkaround Wrap to Cradle with Deney Terrio Double Unwind [MDT]**.

∞

Lead's Cradle, Follow's Inside Turn [MLC]

Lead straight into Lead's Cradle (p. 126), traveling forward along LOD for two bars. On the second (2), the Lead initiates a Pivaloop, using his right hand to send the Follow into an inside turn under her left arm. She steps forward R on (2), and backs across LOD on (3). Complete the turn and end facing in, holding the hand that you need for the circle.

If you start the turn earlier, on (6), it can be a **Lead's Cradle with Pivaloop Free Spin** [MLF].

∞

Tripled Single Pivots [MTP]

Leads, don't just throw this one on anyone, but if your new partner is someone you know well, Tripled Single Pivots (p. 103) is a particularly sweet mixer variation. Those twelve short counts in your partner's arms almost seem longer when you get three rotations instead of two.

∞

Invent Your Own

Invent your own four bar sequence that naturally resolves with the Follow at the Lead's right, both facing into the center of the circle holding right-to-left hands. It's tricky, but fun when you find something that flows smoothly.

A couple of important notes for Leads about this:

- Work out each new variation *before* you dance it in the mixer, rather than using each new partner as a guinea pig to perfect a half-baked idea. Not only is it unsatisfying for your partner when things don't work out, but the other dancers near you are also relying on you and your partner to be in the right place at the right time. So be sure that your new invention will work out before you lead it in the mixer.

- In addition to making it work out, you also want to make it satisfying for your partner. These four bars will form her sole impression of you, so make it a good one. Make sure whatever you lead is comfortable for her, and easy to follow on the fly. In addition, consider how sociable the variation feels. For example, while He Goes, She Goes fits in four bars, and allows you to sweep her into the circle, her first impression of you would essentially be you ditching her.

- Note that each time you dance the sequence, you're dancing with someone new, so there's no reason you need to come up with a new variation every time. Even if you lead the same variation over and over again, each Follow you meet will experience it as something new (and you'll also have a new experience, since each Follow has their own unique style). So maybe just work on perfecting one mixer variation at a time, rather than trying to do something new with each partner.

∞

Two Turning Basics [MTT]

Sometimes the simplest is the best. Enjoy the short time you have together with this partner.

Chapter 30

Advantages of Cross-Step Waltz

At Stanford and UT, we teach our students a wide variety of dances, including swing dances, Latin dances, vintage dances, and waltzes. But when we ask our students which dance is their favorite, the most common response is Cross-Step Waltz.

What is it that makes Cross-Step Waltz so appealing?

Innovation

Some dances, particularly competition dances, have a defined syllabus of acceptable variations. Inventing your own moves is therefore frowned upon. (For a fictionalized example of this, see the movie "Strictly Ballroom.")

Cross-Step Waltz is just the opposite: as a dance, it explicitly encourages innovation. From the beginning, creativity has been an essential part of Cross-Step Waltz's DNA, and this is still the case today. When a student shows us a new move in Cross-Step Waltz and asks, "Is this a move in Cross-Step Waltz?" our response is invariably, "It is now!"

In addition to encouraging innovation, Cross-Step Waltz makes it easy to innovate. In most waltzes, like Box Step, Rotary, and Viennese, a dancer steps directly into his or her partner on (1), in a closed frame, which means you often need to use a specialized maneuver to break out of the frame. In Cross-Step Waltz, on the other hand, the dancers begin by walking forward side-by-side, which makes it easier to break out of the frame into a variety of different kinds of figures right at the beginning.

Another important part of creating a new variation is figuring out how to exit out of it and return back to the basic step. In other waltzes, you have to align exactly to allow one partner to step directly into the other. But in Cross-Step Waltz, you only need to return to your partner's side, without intertwined footwork. This makes even the trickiest figures easy to recover from in Cross-Step Waltz. Even if you happen to get on the wrong foot, it's easy to see your partner's cross-step and mirror it, immediately getting back in sync with them.

Another aspect of Cross-Step Waltz that encourages innovation is its easy-going walking tempo. While the faster tempo of Viennese Waltz and the slower tempo of Box Step Waltz require you to think carefully about your footwork, the walking tempo of Cross-Step Waltz allows you to flow easily through each figure with natural walking steps. This also makes Cross-Step Waltz one of the most relaxing dances, one that you can dance for hours without getting tired.

Full Range of Complexity

Some dances are easy to learn, like Four-Count Street Swing, but remain too easy to hold the interest of advanced dancers. On a difficulty scale of 1-to-10, the entire range of the dance is only 1 to 4.

Other dance forms are so difficult that beginners find them hard to even start. The difficulty of Argentine Tango or West Coast Swing might range from 4 to 10, with an initial difficulty level of 4 feeling overwhelming to a beginner.

Cross-Step Waltz is the best of both, spanning the full range from 1 to 10. Beginners find themselves traveling around the floor successfully in their first lesson, and the most experienced dancers are still challenged at the most advanced levels, years later.

Dual Modes

Some social dances, like the original Rotary Waltz, are comprised of one basic step repeated. Enthusiasts call this "trance-like." Other dances, like Salsa and Tango, are comprised of a series of constantly-changing figures. Enthusiasts call this "exhilarating."

Cross-Step Waltz can be danced in either mode, as the Lead chooses, or as the Lead senses that the Follow prefers. Doing no variations other than the Turning Basic for three minutes can be sublimely satisfying. But a highly active succession of figures can also be a blast. And shifting from one paradigm to the other offers great variety and contrast.

∞

There are many other reasons why our students give for why they particularly enjoy dancing Cross-Step Waltz. It travels, it rotates, and it has beautiful music. But the advantages described above are some of the most compelling reasons that have been cited for why Cross-Step Waltz is *uniquely* satisfying, and why it has such widespread and enduring appeal.

Chapter 31

Creativity in Cross-Step Waltz

It's fun to learn and dance the classic variations. But it's also fun to create your own. In this chapter, we'll share some tips for creating new Cross-Step Waltz variations.

In the "Creativity" chapter of our first book, *Waltzing*, we discussed the creative process in general. For the sake of efficiency, in this chapter, we'll focus on some new ideas related to creating Cross-Step Waltz variations.

Lessons from the Waltz Lab

Many of the tips in this chapter come from our experience running and participating in the Waltz Lab. The Waltz Lab was a project that Richard started at Google and continued at Stanford, in which dancers from around the country worked together to create new waltz variations each week.

Constrain Yourself

Our first piece of advice may seem like an odd one. But by putting limits on your creativity, you'll actually find it much easier to be creative. In practical terms, it's easier to come up with "a new Grapevine variation in Cross-Step Waltz" than it is to come up with "a new variation in Cross-Step Waltz." While this may seem counterintuitive, research in a variety of different fields has found that constraints lead to creativity.

For this reason, most weeks of the Waltz Lab were given a theme: grapevines, shadow position, tango-inspired variations, etc. But every once in a while, there was a wildcard week with no theme. As one of the most prolific creators in the Waltz Lab, Nick can confirm that it was *much* easier to come up with variations during the themed weeks than it was during the wildcard weeks because it's easier to work from the seed of an idea than a blank slate.

Therefore, rather than just trying to come up with "something new," give yourself constraints to create within. One easy way to do this is to try to come up with a new variation that fits into one of the existing families of variations, i.e., pick a specific chapter of this book to work in: He Goes, Cradle Position, Endings, etc. Or make all of the existing families off-limits, and try to come up with a new family entirely.

Riff on Something

In the Waltz Lab, creators were encouraged to riff on each other's ideas, coming up with their own versions of each other's variations. This is essentially another kind of creative constraint that says "create something like this, but not exactly like this." For example, the Pivoting Five-Count Grapevine (p. 49) was based on an original idea by Susan de Guardiola that was refined by Richard, crafted into another form by Nick and Melissa, then taken further with group feedback at one of Richard's Berea Waltz Weekends.

To do this, pick an existing variation, and see if you can improve upon it. As you dance the variation, think "what about this variation could be better—more comfortable, more efficient, more interesting, etc.?" Once you've identified something that could use improvement, try to come up with ways to make it better, while keeping the parts of the variation you like.

Adapt Something

In addition to borrowing from other dancers, you can also borrow from other dances. Many Cross-Step Waltz variations were originally adaptations of popular figures from other dances like Tango, Swing, and Salsa.

Therefore, if there's a variation you like in another dance that doesn't yet have an equivalent in Cross-Step Waltz, see if you can find a way to adapt it, or some elements of it, to make it work in Cross-Step Waltz.

A good first step to adapting a variation into Cross-Step Waltz is to identify what it is about your chosen variation that makes it unique. For example, regardless of what dance you put it in, Pretzel is always going to involve a particular sequence of turns.

Once you've identified the key part of your chosen variation, find a way to get into it: the easiest way to do this is simply to find a time in an existing Cross-Step Waltz variation where you're already doing the beginning of the figure, or are in a convenient place to start it. For example, to put Pretzel into Cross-Step Waltz, find a place where you're already doing Matador, and lead into Pretzel from there.

Next, do the variation, adapting the timing, orientation, footwork, and/or styling as necessary to fit it into Cross-Step Waltz. This will probably require some experimentation.

Finally, find an elegant way to get out of it, perhaps by leading into one of the common endings that are shared by existing variations in Cross-Step Waltz (more on this in a bit).

Try Something Random

During the Waltz Lab, our friend Lucas Garron wrote a script called the Random Dance Move Generator which randomly generates the names of dance moves by mashing up various pieces of dance vocabulary. You can find an updated version of this generator that we've designed specifically for Cross-Step Waltz at: crossstepwaltz.com/random

Each time you click the button, a random name for a Cross-Step Waltz variation will be generated. While some are a bit crazy (e.g., "back-led windmill followed by role-reversed pivots which resolves to behind-the-back neck roll"), others, such as "zig-zag grapevine" or "continuous matador" can inspire new variations.

Here are a few tips for using the Random Cross-Step Waltz Move Generator:

1. Persevere! 9 out of 10 suggestions may sound ridiculous, but if you keep on clicking, you'll eventually find something promising.

2. Even if something sounds ridiculous, there may still be potential, so give it a chance before you dismiss it out of hand. At the same time, don't worry if you can't make it work: there's always another possibility just a click away!

3. You don't have to use the whole name: just focus on the part that sounds promising. For example, in the long example above, you could play with the idea of "role-reversed pivots" without worrying about the "back-led windmill" or "behind-the-back neck roll."

When using the Random Cross-Step Waltz Move Generator, it's important to note that the Generator doesn't invent new variations: you do! The Generator simply provides the necessary constraints to unlock your natural creativity as a dancer.

The Random Cross-Step Waltz Move Generator is great for mashing up existing Cross-Step Waltz vocabulary, but it's also possible to create new vocabulary. In other words, many years ago, someone was the first to discover the ways of moving that we now call "Cradle," "Matador," and "Tornado." You too can be the first to discover a new way of moving!

To help you discover new ways of moving, we've created a second version of the Random Generator that generates potential names for dance moves that don't exist yet. Every time you click the button, it will give you a new word or phrase that has the potential to inspire new ways of moving. For example, what does "about-face" look like in Cross-Step Waltz? How about "Cupid's bow" or "double agent"? (If you're wondering where all these names came from, Nick spent several days reading the dictionary cover to cover, combing through 150,000 entries to generate a list of the 1,000 most promising words and phrases.)

As before, the purpose of this generator is simply to provide you with constraints to inspire your natural creativity. Even if the final variation looks nothing like the name that inspired it, that's okay—the purpose of the name is simply to start you down the path to finding something new, not to limit you once you're on that path.

You can find the Random Dance Vocabulary Generator at: crossstepwaltz.com/vocab

Edit

Often, the first form of a new variation isn't yet the best one. Therefore, it's important to edit.

As you dance the variation, look for ways you might be able to improve it: can you make it more comfortable, more efficient, or more interesting? Try several different versions and see which one works the best.

After editing the figure with your initial creative partner, it's a good idea to dance it with other people as well (Leads, you can lead other Follows into it, and Follows, you can teach it to other Leads). Then ask them what they like and dislike about it and whether they have any ideas to improve it. Both of these questions are important, as what they like and dislike is good to know even if they don't immediately have ideas to improve it.

While getting feedback from different partners, always be respectful and receptive. Sometimes, a defensive Lead will argue with a Follow about her own perspective (or vice versa). But until you've danced your new variation in the opposite role, you don't know what's comfortable for that role. And even if you have danced it in the opposite role and think it's fine, you want to know what someone else finds uncomfortable so you can make it even better. In any case, if you dance both roles, it's a good idea to dance your new variation as both a Lead and a Follow so you can see how well it works on both sides.

Constructing Variations

While it's useful to know these big-picture strategies for creating variations, it's also useful to know the nitty-gritty details of how Cross-Step Waltz variations are constructed.

Like any good story, a good Cross-Step Waltz variation has a beginning, middle, and end. In general, you'll break out of the Turning Basic, do something different, and finish by returning to the Turning Basic.

The Beginning

There are a variety of different ways you can break out of a Turning Basic. Here are just a few of the most common:

- He Goes on (1).
- Grapevine on (1).
- Stopping on (1) or (2).
- Inside Turn on (2).
- Cross-Body Inside Turn on (2).
- Pivots on (2).
- Waterfall Grapevine on (4).
- Coda Pivot on (5).

The Middle

Once you've broken out of the Turning Basic, see what you can do from there. You'll find that each Beginning has different kinds of Middles that flow naturally from it. So if your desired Middle doesn't work from one Beginning, try another way into it.

Whatever the Middle may be, if it involves turns, make sure they happen on the correct (i.e., comfortable) foot. In particular, note that in a CW turn, you pivot forward R and back L, and in a CCW turn, you pivot forward L and back R. Therefore, you can step forward R or back L into a CW turn, or forward L or back R into a CCW turn. And *not* vice versa!

The End

As you're dancing the Middle, look for opportunities to seamlessly transition back into the Turning Basic. How you do this will depend on which lane you're in. Here are just a few of the most common endings from each lane:

Follow on the Inside Lane

- Sweep across LOD on (4).
- Pivaloop Free Spin on (1).

Follow on the Outside Lane

- Outside Turn on (4).
- Double Outside Turn on (2).

Of course, the turns can also be free spins or rollaways (and vice versa).

Whether you finish with one of these popular endings, or something else, it's important to make sure that both partners are set up to cross into the primary cross-step on (1), or to seamlessly transition into another variation.

The Follow's Role in Creativity

Whenever we teach creativity classes, there are usually some Follows who tell us that they don't know how to contribute to the process of creating new variations. "The Lead comes up with things, and I just follow them, so creating variations isn't really my job." There's so much to unpack here, but for now, we'll simply say that we completely disagree. There are many different ways that Follows can contribute to the process of creating new variations.

First, as we noted before, it's essential for both roles to weigh in on a new variation to make sure it's satisfying from both perspectives. So at the very least, when a new variation is created (by a dancer in either role), it's essential for a Follow to serve as an editor. There are far too many examples of Lead-created variations that seem to work from the Lead's perspective, but are terrible from the Follow's.

It's important to note that editing as a Follow is different from following in general (just as editing as a Lead is different from leading in general). A good Follow can make even a bad variation look good: when editing, the Follow needs to step out of this adaptive mindset for a moment and see where things are going wrong, or could potentially go wrong. Rather than making it work, let it fail! In doing so, you'll help the Lead identify opportunities for improvement and make the resulting creation even better.

Once we explain this part of the process, most Follows embrace their role as editor. But some see this as their only role: "Oh, I get it: he generates new ideas, and I tell him which are good ones and bad ones." Once again, we disagree. In fact, if pressed to choose which role is better positioned to come up with new variations, we might even say it's the Follow role.

Why? First of all, in most variations, the focus is on the Follow and what's comfortable for her. And who is better to say what's comfortable for her than her? While an experienced Lead can *analyze* what's most comfortable for his partner, his partner *knows* this intuitively, and can identify opportunities that the Lead might miss.

Similarly, the best variations are those in which the Follow's next step is exactly what she expects it to be. Therefore, while slowly dancing through the variation, if the Follow asks herself "what comes next?" her answer is probably what the variation should be.

Another huge advantage of creating as a Follow is that Follows generally have a larger vocabulary than Leads. For the most part, Leads only get to dance what they already know, while Follows are regularly led into new things by Leads who have different vocabularies. This means that a Follow generally has a more complete picture of what's possible in a dance than any one Lead. This gives her a great advantage when it comes to piecing together new variations: she knows more ways of entering and exiting certain positions, more things that can happen in each position, etc. If she can figure out how to tap into this knowledge, the average Follow has more raw material for creativity than the average Lead.

This advantage also has the potential to be a disadvantage because it can make the Follow more likely to dismiss something by thinking "oh, I've already seen that one before." But creativity is coming up with something new to you, not something that has never been thought of before. So celebrate your own (and your partner's) creations, even if they feel familiar.

Share Your Findings

If you come up with something new in Cross-Step Waltz and want to share, let us know at: crossstepwaltz.com/share

Chapter 32

Role Reversal in Cross-Step Waltz

In *Waltzing*, we talked about the benefits of role reversal, i.e., dancing as a Lead if you usually Follow, or vice versa. To summarize, role reversal:

- allows us to experience the whole dance, not just half of it
- increases our empathy and appreciation for our partner, as we discover that their role is actually more challenging than we might've thought
- improves our own partnering by showing us what works (and doesn't) for the other role
- provides a healthy mental challenge
- lets us decide which role(s) we want to dance based on first-hand experience with both roles, rather than traditional assumptions about gender

And most importantly, role reversal is fun!

We also noted that the symmetry and easygoing creativity of Cross-Step Waltz make it a particularly easy dance to reverse roles in. In this chapter, you'll learn exactly why this is and how to easily reverse roles on the fly.

Why It's Easy

The main reason role reversal is easy in Cross-Step Waltz is that to reverse roles in a Turning Basic, you don't need to change the feet. All you need to do is change the arms, taking role-reversed position. From there, keep dancing the exact same steps, helping each other through the rotation as you normally do. While your handhold has changed, the way you get around your partner (and help them get around you) is exactly the same. In other words, if you can dance a Turning Basic without touching, as in the Innovation (p. 18), you can also dance it while holding each other in a slightly different position.

Note: If the Lead was dancing Waterfall, he'll want to switch over to crossing in front instead of behind. Similarly, the Follow may want to switch over to crossing behind for Waterfall, but this isn't a necessity, just an option.

Another reason role reversal is easy in Cross-Step Waltz is that all you need is the Turning Basic. In other dances, if role reversal is limited to the basic step, both dancers are going to be bored. But if it involves leading and following other variations, both dancers are going to be challenged (which can certainly be fun, but it can also be stressful). In Cross-Step Waltz, on the other hand, a role-reversed Turning Basic is satisfying enough as it is, while also being nice and easy, so it's a great introduction to role reversal.

Then, if the new Lead does want to try leading variations, both roles already know most of the footwork involved. Most common variations that the new Lead might try will use footwork that both roles already know from dancing their own role in similar variations. For example, if the new Lead leads a Grapevine Outside Turn, they both generally know how to dance a partnered Grapevine, and the new Follow already knows the outside turn footwork from the rollaway on the outside lane that he's used to doing in He Goes, Rollaway. All that's really changed is the arms, but even those are usually mirrored, and each role just needs to imitate the timing and techniques they've come to appreciate in their usual partners. This is as opposed to many other dances, in which almost everything about the roles, from the feet to the arms, is different.

More than just being easy because we know it from the opposite role, the footwork of Cross-Step Waltz is easier than other dances in general. Rather than having complicated footwork patterns and timings, Cross-Step Waltz is almost entirely based on four easy kinds of walking steps: cross-steps, side steps, forward steps, and backing steps, which, 95% of the time, are taken one step per beat. Therefore, as long as you're falling into the most natural step at the moment, you're probably doing it right. Given that both roles have lots of experience doing this in their own role, it's easy to translate this skill into the opposite role, where you're doing exactly the same thing in a different context.

One final benefit of role reversal in Cross-Step Waltz is that the music is slower, at a comfortable walking tempo. This gives both partners a chance to puzzle things out together, rather than having to know each part before attempting it, as you would if the music were faster.

How to Do It

Given how easy and fun role reversal is in Cross-Step Waltz, dancers have come up with many different ways of role reversing on the fly, the best of which we'll describe now.

In general, the variations will be divided into two different categories: variations in which the Lead gives the lead over, and variations in which the Follow steals the lead.

Giving the Lead

Leads, before you lead any of these variations, ask the Follow if she'd like to lead, rather than just throwing her into it. While role reversal is fun, it's also optional, for when both partners want to reverse roles.

Timing Note: In most transitions, you'll end up dancing on the (4) rather than the (1). If you want to dance on the (1), you can dance a Stop and Go (p. 20) to shift the downbeat.

Position Note: When taking role-reversed position, make sure the new Lead's left hand is underneath, more horizontal, and the new Follow's right hand is on top, more vertical. Some people remember to change the arms but forget to change the hands.

∞

Orbits to Role Reversal [ORR]

(1-2-3) As in Orbits (p. 17), the Lead tosses himself across in front of the Follow to the outside lane. But rather than placing his left arm under hers, he places his left arm over hers, with his left hand on top of her right shoulder, then offers his right hand to her. She takes his right hand in her left, in role-reversed position, with the Follow leading.

Hint: This works better when the Lead transfers his left arm first, and then offers his right hand, rather than trying to change both hands at once.

(4-5-6) The start of a Turning Basic with the Follow leading and the Lead following.

The footwork flows effortlessly, without stopping.

A benefit of this transition is that it can be used to nonverbally offer the Follow the lead without requiring her to take it. If she wants to lead, she takes role-reversed position. If she doesn't, she simply Orbits herself across, placing her left hand back on top of his shoulder, which politely communicates to him that she'd like to keep following.

∞

Waist Slide to Role Reversal [WSR]

The idea of using a Waist Slide to reverse roles has been explored by many different dancers over the years. Here's a simple and elegant way to do it:

(1-2-3) A Waist Slide (p. 37), but as the Follow flies by the Lead's left side, he offers her his right hand in role-reversed position, as his left arm naturally passes on top of her right.

(4-5-6) The start of a Turning Basic with the Follow leading and the Lead following.

In this and other transitions, if she doesn't immediately realize she's leading now, the old Lead may need to continue leading (back-leading) for a bar or two until it's clear that it's a role-reversed Turning Basic and she picks up the lead.

∞

Lead's Cradle to Role Reversal [LCR]

This idea has also been explored by many different dancers. Here's the basic concept:

Get into Lead's Cradle (p. 126), then the Lead gives himself an outside turn on (1-2-3), passing the lead over to the Follow for a Turning Basic on (4-5-6).

You can either go straight into Lead's Cradle, or you can stop in Lead's Cradle during Chained Cradle (p. 124).

∞

Two and Half Pivots to Role Reversal [TPR]

This variation was invented by Kevin Hsu and Jane Huang during the Waltz Lab.

(1-2-3-4) A Single Pivot: "cross-pivot-pivot-walk."

(5-6-1-2-3) A Pivot and a Half: "cross-pivot-pivot-pivot-walk." Going into this Pivot and a Half, switch to a modified Barrel Hold, holding each other's shoulders with both left arms over both right arms, then peel open to role-reversed position at the end.

(4-5-6) The start of a Turning Basic with the Follow leading and the Lead following.

∞

Shadow Sombrero to Role Reversal [STR]

Lead the Sombrero exit from Shadow (p. 145), then toss yourself across into role-reversed position on (1-2-3).

While it's really no different than Orbits to Role Reversal, it feels particularly natural here because in Sombrero, his right arm is above her left one, so it makes sense that he'd toss his left arm on top of her right one into role-reversed position.

Crossed-Hand Sombrero to Role Reversal [CSO]

This was invented by Acata Felton and Mirage Marrou Greene during the Waltz Lab.

(1-2-3) He Goes (p. 33).

(4-5-6) As you walk forward along LOD, pass the Follow's right hand into the Lead's right and take left hands under.

(1-2-3) As you continue to walk forward, lead the double face loop of Sombrero, passing the right hands over his head and the left hands over hers.

(4-5-6) The Lead offers his right hand to the Follow's left in role-reversed position and sends her into the first half of a Turning Basic with the Follow leading.

∞

Brake Step Role Reversal [BSR]

This role reversal variation is unique in that it doesn't require you to dance Stop and Go to shift the downbeat: the phase-shifting happens as part of the variation itself.

(1-2-3) The first half of the Brake Step (p. 107), i.e., cross (1), block the Follow with a step straight back along LOD for the Lead and straight forward along LOD for the Follow (2), rock/replace against LOD (3), starting to rotate CW.

(4-5-6) Continue your CW rotation into a side step against LOD (4), holding (5), and a small side step along LOD (6). Change the left-to-right hands over on the first side step, and the right-to-left hands on the second side step, leading into a Follow-led Turning Basic on (1). Given how quickly this all happens, the Lead will definitely want to back-lead the first Turning Basic in order to help ease the Follow into her new role.

∞

Stealing the Lead

Follows, if you know your partner is game to follow, there are also a variety of ways that you can steal the lead from him.

∞

Backled Orbits to Role Reversal [BOR]

At the beginning of a Turning Basic, disengage the held hands and send the Lead strongly across LOD in front of you with your left arm as in Orbits, tossing his left hand to your right shoulder and taking role-reversed position, then lead into a role-reversed Turning Basic on (4).

Rollaway Steal to Role Reversal [RSR]

This basic concept has been discovered by many different innovators over the years.

Anytime there's a rollaway with the Follow on the inside lane (as in He Goes, Rollaway), the Follow can take the Lead in role-reversed position and lead into a Turning Basic on (4-5-6).

Follows: He'll probably be expecting to take inside hands and sweep you across LOD, but if you get ahead of him and confidently offer role-reversed position, he'll probably take it, and may not even immediately realize that you've stolen the lead.

It can also be done after a free spin on the inside lane, but the rollaway makes it a little easier since his back is turned to you while you're getting ahead of him.

∞

Lead's Flip into Role Reversed Shadow [LFR]

In this Waltz Lab variation, the Follow seamlessly sends the Lead from the Lead role in closed position into the Follow role in Shadow Position.

(1-2-3) Using her right hand (and his left), the Follow starts to lead a mirrored version of a Cross-Body Inside Turn, bringing his left hand into the frame and passing it into her left as he flips across LOD to the outside lane, and taking right-in-right into Shadow Position with the Lead in front on the right. The Follow is now leading and the Lead is following.

(4-5-6) The Follow is free to lead Shadow variations from there, or she can use any Shadow exit to send the Lead into the Follow role in a Turning Basic.

∞

Shadow Steal to Role Reversal [SSR]

A variety of steals from Shadow Position have been experimented with over the years.

When the Lead is in front in Shadow Position, either after the above variation, or halfway through Mixmaster (p. 139), the Follow can lead any of the exits from Shadow on the Lead.

For example, the Follow leads a Face Loop from Shadow (p. 144) on the Lead on (1-2-3), starting a Turning Basic on (4-5-6).

Mixmaster Steal to Role Reversal [MSR]

If the Lead has the Follow in Shadow, and the Follow wants to steal the lead, she can lead the Follow's Flip in Front to Shadow (p. 139) to flip the Lead in front, then lead Shadow variations or a Shadow exit to a Turning Basic.

A particularly surprising and satisfying option is to flip him in front on (5) and keep turning him (6-1-2-3) straight into a Face Loop exit to a Turning Basic. The footwork is similar to the Superspeed version of Mixmaster (p. 140), but with the Lead doing the Follow's part.

Cradle Steal to Role Reversal [CDR]

Cradle has also commonly been used for role reversal. Here's a particularly nice steal.

When the Follow is in Cradle Position, she can lead the Lead into a Pivaloop Free Spin.

With her right hand to his left, she leads him into a Pivaloop across in front of her on (4-5-6), and a free spin in the outside lane on (1-2-3). Then she catches him in role-reversed position for a Turning Basic on (4-5-6).

Note: If the Lead happens to be in Lead's Cradle, the Follow can lead him into one of the many Follow's Cradle exits, but Lead's Cradle is relatively rare, so this steal from Follow's Cradle is more practical.

In all of these role reversal variations, verbal leads are also allowed, like a playful "You're following now!" as she's stealing the lead.

Switch Dancing

"Lead, Follow, or Switch?"

In the past, there were only two roles in social dancing: Lead and Follow. But with the recent growth in interest in role reversal, many dancers have become "ambidancetrous"—a portmanteau of "dance" and "ambidextrous"—meaning they're comfortable dancing either role.

When two ambidancers dance with each other, there are a variety of different possibilities: A leads and B follows; B leads and A follows; or A and B switch roles throughout the dance. This third option is known as "Switch."

As we noted before, Cross-Step Waltz is a particularly easy dance to reverse roles in, both because of the structure of the dance itself, and the ease with which the lead can be passed back and forth through a variety of elegant role reversal variations. This makes it an ideal vehicle for Switch.

To dance Switch in Cross-Step Waltz, first, ask your partner if they'd like to. "Lead, Follow, or Switch?" is a common way to ask which role your partner would like to dance. (If "Switch" isn't yet a common term in your community, you may need to explain what this means.)

Then decide who's going to lead and follow first. Here's a particularly elegant way to ask someone whether they want to lead or follow non-verbally: after you've asked them to dance, as you're about to take hands, offer both hands, left palm up and right palm down. If they want to lead, they'll take your right hand with their left hand palm up (swingout hands with them leading), and if they want to follow, they'll take your left hand with their right hand palm down (swingout hands with you leading). This method can be used to determine whether your partner wants to lead or follow first in a Switch dance, or whether your partner wants to lead or follow in a traditional Lead/Follow dance.

Then, once you're dancing, in addition to leading and following any number of normal variations, the current Lead looks for ways to give the lead over to the current Follow, and/or the current Follow looks for ways to steal the lead. In either case, work together to keep the dance flowing seamlessly the whole time. The transitions should be so smooth that anyone who happens to be watching—and maybe even the dancers themselves—don't even notice where the points of transition are. Then, as a further ideal, see if you can do it musically, matching the change in roles to a change in the music.

Important Caveat

In talking about Switch dancing, it's important to note that just because it's new and different doesn't necessarily make it better. Switch dancing is fun, but so is traditional Lead/Follow dancing. Sometimes you may feel like dancing Switch, and other times you may prefer leading or following. All three modes are equally good.

Chapter 33

Analogies for Leading and Following

At UT Austin, Nick and Melissa ensure role-balance in their classes by having two different sections of each class, a Leads section and a Follows section. Every semester, prospective beginners email us to ask what the difference is. "What is a Lead?" they ask, "and what is a Follow?"

Over the years, we've found that it's much easier to lead and follow (and to teach people how to lead and follow) than it is to explain what leading and following are. But in this chapter, we'll try to do just that with the help of three analogies for leading and following. But first, we need to deconstruct a bad analogy.

If you ask Google what leading and following are, you'll get some *interesting* responses. For example, here's what the first hit, a blog post from a major franchised dance studio, has to say:

> As a happily married man I know that my wife is truly in charge, but she's smart enough to let me feel in charge when we're on the dance floor. As a man it's an awesome rush when your partner does whatever you ask, with elegance and poise. A great follower enjoys the ride. When dancing a Waltz it's kind of like riding shotgun in a smooth Cadillac and Salsa is like speeding down the road in a limber Porsche. The follower gets to enjoy the ride while the leader gets to press all of the buttons.

Examples like this—of which there are many more—really get our blood boiling, not only because they're offensive, but also because they're inaccurate. In this analogy, and others like it, the Follow is portrayed as being entirely passive, with no voice whatsoever in the dance. That isn't the dynamic of truly social dancing.

Note: Our message is not that most people currently dance this way, but shouldn't. It's that most people don't actually dance this way. Although there are still some dancers who agree with that "happily married man," we're now living in the 21st century, when most people prefer the more egalitarian dynamic of truly social dancing.

So if this isn't how people actually dance, what's a better way of explaining how they do?

As a start, let's begin with with the literal definitions. According to the most relevant senses of these two words in the Oxford English Dictionary, to lead means "to accompany and show the way to; to conduct, guide, esp. to direct or guide by going on in advance; to cause to follow in one's path." To follow means "to go forward along (a path), to keep in (a track) as one goes."

Dancing Down the Ski Slope

Based on these definitions, a good analogy that comes to mind for following is snowboarding through a terrain park, interacting with features created by the Lead. While the terrain features constrain a snowboarder's choice of tricks—jumps are for aerial tricks, and rails are for jibbing (i.e., sliding)—the snowboarder decides exactly how to execute them. Similarly, while the Lead defines the basic shape of the figures, the Follow actively decides how to execute them, and in doing so, creates the dance.

Following is like snowboarding through a terrain park

Note: We're not the first to come up with this analogy for following. For an eloquent explanation from the perspective from one of our students, see Anne-Laure's essay on p. 191.

The fact that the Lead provides constraints is what enables the Follow to do what she does. In the snowboarding analogy, the terrain features are what enable the tricks. While there are some tricks you can do on a flat slope, terrain features enable a snowboarder to do a far greater variety of tricks, just as dancing with a Lead enables a Follow to dance a far greater variety of variations. In addition, having a particular "terrain feature" in front of them frees the

Follow to focus on executing a particular variety of trick at the moment, rather than having to choose from all possibilities.

This is a good analogy for following, but it's not a particularly good one for leading. (As far as we know, there aren't any on-the-fly terrain park creators that actively adapt the terrain features to the current riders, although that would be awesome!)

So what is leading?

Dancing & Dragons

As an analogy that works for both leading and following, consider a game of Dungeons and Dragons (D&D), where the Lead is the Dungeon Master (DM), and the Follow is a player. In D&D, the DM defines the shape of the adventure, and guides the player through it. But while the DM puts constraints on the player, they don't actually control what the player does. Instead, they create scenarios for the player, and the player decides how to respond.

Social dancing is like playing D&D

This is exactly how leading and following works in social dancing: the Lead defines the shape of the dance, and guides the Follow through it. But while the Lead gives the Follow guidelines, they don't actually control what the Follow does. Instead, they create scenarios for the Follow, and the Follow decides how to respond.

In a good game of D&D, there is a mutual respect between the DM and the player. When the DM gives the player a scenario, the player respects that scenario and builds on it. When the DM says there's a door in front of them, the player respects that, and interacts with the door. But however the player chooses to interact with the door—picking the lock, taking an axe to it, or burning it down with a spell—the DM respects that and provides the next logical step in their mutually-created storyline.

Similarly, when the Lead leads the Follow into something, the Follow respects that, and follows his lead. But however the Follow interprets his lead, the Lead respects that, and provides the next logical step in their mutually-created choreography.

Chapter 34

Creative Interpretations

As we've noted before, Cross-Step Waltz is a naturally creative dance. In addition to experimenting within the form, dancers have also experimented with the form itself. This chapter includes some of those creative interpretations.

Reverse Cross-Step Waltz

This is simply Cross-Step Waltz that turns to the left instead of the right. Here's the basic:

Reverse Turning Basic [RTB]

(1) Primary cross-step, but this time, the Follow is slightly winning the race along LOD.

(2) The Follow backs around CCW with her R as the Lead steps straight forward L along LOD between her feet.

(3) Both step along LOD.

(4-5-6) The Follow does what the Lead did on (1-2-3), and vice versa.

∞

Reverse Waterfall [RWF]

Some dancers find it more comfortable to do a Reverse Waterfall, with the Follow crossing behind on (4), just as the Lead does on (4) of Waterfall (p. 16). As in Waterfall, this is an optional styling chosen by the dancer crossing behind, which in this case is the Follow. (If the Lead crossed behind, it would break the frame in the same way as the Follow crossing behind on the fourth count of a regular Turning Basic would.)

Reverse Cross-Step Waltz is most commonly done as a variation of traditional Cross-Step Waltz, dancing a few left-turning Basics between your normal right-turning Basics.

But for the more adventurous, you can stay in Reverse Cross-Step Waltz for longer, and see what variations you can do in this new dance.

∞

Some variations can be done just as they are in Cross-Step Waltz, for example:

Zig-Zag in Reverse Cross-Step Waltz [RZZ]

From a Reverse Turning Basic, send the Follow in front of the Lead into Zig-Zag (p. 87), then recommence a Reverse Turning Basic on any (1).

∞

Other variations can be adapted to Reverse Cross-Step Waltz simply by turning them to the left, and switching who backs around first, as in:

Reverse Tripled Single Pivots [RTP]

This is simply a left-turning version of Tripled Single Pivots (p. 103).

Cross (1), Follow backing pivot (2), Lead backing pivot (3), walk along LOD (4), and repeat two more times, for three complete left pivots in twelve counts. Then recommence a Reverse Turning Basic.

Theoretically, Reverse Tripled Single Pivots could also be danced in traditional Cross-Step Waltz, but they're much more comfortable in Reverse Cross-Step Waltz because you're already turning left. This not only means they're easier to get into; it also means that you avoid jolting straight from the third CCW pivot into a CW Turning Basic, as you would if you attempted it in traditional Cross-Step Waltz.

∞

Similarly, if you're dancing Reverse Cross-Step Waltz and lead a variation you know from regular Cross-Step Waltz which resolves in a CW turn for the Follow, you'll often find that it's more comfortable to transition into regular Cross-Step Waltz afterwards rather than trying to go straight from this CW turn to a Reverse Turning Basic. This means that many variations can be used as dramatic transitions from Reverse Cross-Step Waltz to Cross-Step Waltz. For example:

Cross-Body Inside Turn and Pivaloop Free Spin to Cross-Step Waltz [RPT]

From Reverse Cross-Step Waltz, lead into a Cross-Body Inside Turn to Pivaloop Free Spin exactly as you know it (p. 29), and you'll naturally find yourself in Cross-Step Waltz at the end.

In addition to variations that elegantly transition *from* Reverse Cross-Step Waltz, there are also variations that elegantly transition *to* it. For example:

Cross-Body Inside Turn to Reverse Cross-Step Waltz [CBR]

From Cross-Step Waltz, start a Cross-Body Inside Turn (p. 29), sending the Follow in front of the Lead to the inside lane, but catch in closed position for the second half of a Reverse Waterfall on (4), meaning that the Follow crosses behind on (4).

If you initiate this turn while already dancing Reverse Cross-Step Waltz, it's an **Inside Turn in Reverse Cross-Step Waltz** [RIT].

∞

There are many more transitions between Cross-Step Waltz and Reverse Cross-Step Waltz, but we'll leave you the satisfaction of discovering them yourself.

∞

Mirror Waltz

Mirror Waltz is a creative form of Cross-Step Waltz in which everything in the dance is mirrored across LOD. The Lead and Follow switch places and dance in mirrored waltz position: the Lead places his left arm under the Follow's right with his left hand on her back, and the right-to-left hands are joined, pointed along LOD. The Lead is on the outside lane and the Follow is on the inside lane. Despite the change in position, the Lead is still leading.

Mirror Turning Basic [MTB]

The basic in Mirror Waltz is essentially a Reverse Turning Basic (p. 183) starting with the Lead in the outside lane (i.e., halfway through the step).

Start in mirrored waltz position, with the Follow's R and Lead's L free. The Follow is on the inside lane and the Lead is on the outside lane.

(1) The Lead crosses L over R as the Follow crosses R over L, with the Lead slightly winning the race along LOD.

(2) The Lead backs around CCW with his R as the Follow steps straight forward L along LOD between his feet.

(3) Both step along LOD.

(4-5-6) The Follow does what the Lead did on (1-2-3), and vice versa.

All variations in Cross-Step Waltz can be adapted into Mirror Waltz: the only difference is that everything is mirrored across LOD. For example, here's He Goes, She Goes in Mirror Waltz. The differences from traditional He Goes, She Goes are italicized:

Mirror He Goes, She Goes [MHG]

(1-2-3) The Lead raises his *right* arm and travels straight forward under it, passing in front of the Follow to the *inside* lane, then lowers his arm, as the Follow crosses trails behind him.

(4-5-6) Both walk forward with the Follow in the *outside* lane. During these steps, the Lead rolls his *right* thumb down, so that his *right* palm is toward his partner.

(1-2-3) He raises his *right* hand and loops it in front of her head into a *CW* Follow's inside turn, as she pivots forward, back, forward, staying in the *outside* lane.

(4-5-6) He lowers his *right* hand and sweeps her by in front of him to the *inside* lane and catches her in *mirror waltz* position, as she crosses strongly forward across in front of him, then pulls her *left* shoulder back to let him get ahead of her for a *Mirror* Turning Basic on (1).

As you can see in the description above, which hands you use, which lanes you're in, and which direction you rotate are all flipped in Mirror Waltz. Left becomes right, outside becomes inside, and CCW becomes CW.

For this reason, dancing Mirror Waltz feels a bit like falling down the rabbit hole into Wonderland: everything is simultaneously familiar, but also completely different.

∞

Mirror Waltz can either be danced from the start as a full dance in its own right, or, like Reverse Cross-Step Waltz, it can be added to traditional Cross-Step Waltz as a variation. Here are some easy transitions between Cross-Step Waltz and Mirror Waltz:

Transition to Mirror Waltz [TMW]

From Cross-Step Waltz, the Lead tosses the Follow across in front of him (p. 87) to the inside lane (1-2-3), taking mirror waltz position and starting Mirror Waltz on (4).

If you want to dance Mirror Waltz on (1), you can do a Stop and Go (p. 20) before transitioning (or a Mirror Stop and Go after transitioning).

∞

Transition from Mirror Waltz [FMW]

From Mirror Waltz, the Lead tosses the Follow across in front of him (1-2-3) to the outside lane, taking waltz position and starting Cross-Step Waltz on (4).

If you shifted the downbeat to dance Mirror Waltz on (1), you'll be dancing Cross-Step Waltz on (4), but you can shift back to (1) by doing a Stop and Go (p. 20) after transitioning (or a Mirror Stop and Go before transitioning).

Innovation Waltzing

In Chapter 3, you learned the basic Innovation (p. 18), which is a Turning Basic without touching your partner. If you're feeling adventurous, you can expand on this concept.

Innovation Waltzing [INW]

Starting from an Innovation Turning Basic, lead and follow other variations without touching, then return to the Innovation Turning Basic.

For example, try an Innovation He Goes, She Goes, with the left-to-right hands floating close to each other, but never touching. Leads, lead everything very clearly, exaggerating all of your signals slightly so she can clearly see them. Follows, since you no longer have a physical lead to interpret, shift your attention to following visually.

Cross-Step Troika

In Russian, *troika* is a carriage drawn by three horses. It's also a folk dance performed by a trio. Taking inspiration from this, Cross-Step Troika is a creative form of Cross-Step Waltz danced by a group of three dancers. It can be done by two Leads and one Follow, two Follows and one Lead, or three dancers who switch roles throughout the dance.

Cutting In [CTI]

In the simplest version, the two dancers of the doubled role take turns dancing with the one dancer of the other role, i.e., Lead 1 dances with the Follow, then Lead 2 does, or Follow 1 dances with the Lead, then Follow 2 does. The video page has videos of our UT Austin class assistants demoing both options.

It's the job of the solo dancer to find elegant times and ways of cutting in (or "stealing," as some dancers call it). This is usually easiest in the middle of a variation. For example, after Lead 1 initiates a turn for the Follow, Lead 2 can swoop in to take her hand and complete the turn. Or while Follow 1 is doing a Free Spin, Follow 2 might step in to dance with the Lead. But if you're clever about it, it's also possible to insert yourself into closed position.

In that vein, here's a particularly nice Troika variation by Don Harvey and friends in Portland, Oregon, which not only switches who's dancing, but also who's leading:

Tripling [TRP]

Consider A who is leading, B who is following, and C who is solo, tracking them on the inside lane. On (1-2-3), C pushes A across LOD in front of B, then takes A in waltz position for a Turning Basic on (4-5-6), with C leading, A following, and B solo. B then changes their feet to the Lead's timing and goes to the inside lane to push C into the Follow role. A, now solo, changes their feet, goes to the inside lane, and pushes B into the Follow role, completing the cycle. Between cut-ins, the two dancing together can do whatever variations they like.

The video makes all of this clear.

∞

Tripling Mixer [TRM]

While making the demo video for Tripling, our class assistant Rissa Jackson had the idea to make a Tripling Mixer, in which a circle of trios all dance Tripling at the same time, and the dancers who are jettisoned from each couple cut in on the next couple that passes by them.

It works best when every opportunity to cut in is taken, i.e., each couple only gets one full Turning Basic together before they are cut in on. The key for the dancers cutting in is to quickly switch your feet and pass behind your previous couple into the inside lane to get ready to cut in on the next couple.

The video shows a poetic trio of trios, but any number of couples can participate.

∞

Another form of Cross-Step Troika has all three people dancing together at the same time:

Trio Waltz [TRI]

There are many different ways you can connect as a trio. For example, you might form:

- a line of three facing along LOD, or
- a circle of three, or
- wrap someone into a three-person Cradle Position by turning that person under one of the hands in a circle and all turning to face the same direction, or
- take the heart-shaped position of the Oklahoma Trio Mixer, with the outside dancers' inside hands joined behind the back of the middle dancer and their outside hands taking the corresponding hand of the middle dancer

In Trio Waltz, the lines between Lead and Follow are necessarily blurred, with everyone leading some and and following some. Get creative!

∞

More than Three [FOR]

If you're feeling particularly adventurous, you can also try dancing with more than three dancers, for a Cross-Step Quartet (or more).

The video shows an adaptation of Orbits for four ("Fourbits").

∞

Cross-Step Waltz Jam (Birthday Dance)

The Cross-Step Waltz Jam, often done to celebrate a birthday or other special occasion, is a form of Cross-Step Waltz in which the dancer being celebrated dances with a number of partners in rapid succession.

Cross-Step Waltz Jam (Birthday Dance) [CWJ]

The potential partners stand in a large circle around the dancer being celebrated, and cut in to dance with them whenever it's convenient, as the tapped-out partner rejoins the circle.

As in Troika, the goal is to cut in in a way that keeps the dance flowing continuously without requiring the celebrated dancer to foot-fudge.

If the celebrated dancer is known to dance both roles, the potential partners can cut in on them in either role.

If there are multiple dancers to celebrate, they can all dance at once: just be sure to have them clearly identify themselves to the group at the beginning of the dance so that the potential partners know who to dance with.

Cross-Step Redowa

Cross-Step Redowa is a mashup of Cross-Step Waltz with the mid-19th century Redowa.

In the original Redowa, (2) and (5) are elongated steps that reach forward and back along LOD. In Cross-Step Redowa, this same elongation occurs on the cross-steps.

To achieve this, the whole dance is shifted one count later than in traditional Cross-Step Waltz, i.e., step 1 is danced on count 2, and so on.

Cross-Step Redowa [CSR]

(1) Leap down into a very short side step along LOD with Lead's L and Follow's R.

(2) Reach along LOD with an elongated cross-step with Lead's R and Follow's L.

(3) The Lead leaps back across LOD with his L as the Follow leaps forward between his feet with his R.

(4-5-6) Repeat opposite to complete the turn.

Apply Redowa styling throughout. (If you don't know what that is, see our detailed description of Redowa in *Waltzing*.)

Cross-Step Redowa is most satisfying when danced to Redowa music, which is faster and more energetic than traditional Cross-Step Waltz music.

Chapter 35

Dancing Down the Ski Slope

An essay by Stanford student Anne-Laure Cuvilliez.

∞

Being a dancer reminds me of skiing. I grew up in a ski resort, which means that skiing became a part of my life. At first, I had to learn every single move, and consciously turn, stabilize myself, then think about the next turn. But slowly I became more proficient, until I didn't need to think about turning, and focused instead on where I wanted to go. Later on, I was able to enjoy the landscape, and the flow of my skiing. Dancing is similar. At first, we need to focus on the steps, but somewhere along the way your focus shifts to your partner, the dancing flow, the music, and other couples dancing.

The comparison does not stop here though. As I mentioned, skiing in my hometown was inherent part of our life. It's a social activity where you meet people, and get to know them, as social dancing is. You can choose to stick to the classical style, or you can experiment with new moves. You can be a show off, or a modest skier. In a similar way to social dancing, the style that works is a good style. It does not need to be the most beautiful way to perform, as long as you enjoy it.

The last similarity is, as a Follow in dance, you need to interpret the signs from your partner. In skiing, your partner is the terrain. You need to interpret the slope, the snow, and navigate the trees and obstacles. In social dance, you interpret the gesture and body position of your partner, and navigate through other couples in the room. I find it relaxing and mentally challenging at the same time. It's relaxing because the Follow doesn't have to decide all the figures and get overwhelmed by the possibilities. On groomed slopes, you have the freedom to go anywhere, but it's boring. I prefer having a more challenging terrain dictating your lines. It makes things more interesting. That's why I prefer being a Follow, because it works in the same way. Instead of being overwhelmed by all the figures possible, and the line of dance, I enjoy interpreting what is going on and responding quickly. It's very relaxing, and at the same time a constant puzzle to solve.

"The art of life lies in a constant
re-adjustment to our surroundings."

— Kakuzo Okakura

Chapter 36

Cross-Step Waltz in Other Timings

Cross-Step Waltz is most commonly danced in 3/4 time at a comfortable walking tempo. But it can also be danced in other timings. In fact, as we saw in Chapter 17, the dance was first done in 4/4 time.

4/4 Time

Originally, Cross-Step Waltz was danced in slow-quick-quick (SQQ) timing to Foxtrot music. The steps are exactly the same, and all the variations work: it's only the timing that's different.

Cross-Step Foxtrot [CSF]

Counts	1	2	3	4	/	1	2	3	4	//	repeat
Steps	1		2	3	/	4		5	6	//	repeat

This works to a wide variety of music, including that which would usually be used for dances like Foxtrot, Nightclub Two Step, Tango, Country Two Step, Schottische, Blues, and more.

∞

Cross-Step Hustle [CSH]

Another option is simply to dance across the music, as in Hustle. In Hustle, the three counts of the dance shift across the four counts of the music. The same can be done with the six counts of Cross-Step Waltz.

Simply dance Cross-Step Waltz in even timing, as you usually do, hearing each beat as a generic beat. For the musically and mathematically inclined, you'll notice that you're shifting across the music, hitting the downbeat with every other primary cross-step (or if you're counting by eights, it will take twice as long).

Counts	1	2	3	4 /	1	2	3	4 /	1	2	3	4	//	repeat
Steps	1	2	3 /	4	5	6 /	1	2	3 /	4	5	6	//	repeat

This also works to a wide variety of music, including that which would usually be used for dances like Hustle, One Step, Polka, and Merengue.

∞

5/4 Time

Music and dancing in 5/4 time is relatively rare, but exists in the form of the 19th century Five Step Waltz, 1910s Half and Half, 1920s Five Step, and contemporary French Valse à 5 Temps. If you happen to have music for those dances, or another tune in 5/4 time, you can dance Cross-Step Waltz like so, using the basic timing of the Half and Half (1—4-5):

Cross-Step Waltz in 5/4 Time [FIV]

Counts	1	2	3	4	5 /	1	2	3	4	5 //	repeat
Steps	1			2	3 /	4			5	6 //	repeat

This is essentially just Cross-Step Foxtrot with an even slower first step, giving three counts to the cross step, instead of the usual two.

∞

7/4 Time

Music and dancing in 7/4 time is rarer still, but existed in the form of the 1914 Tango Moderation and 1930 Seven Step. In the case of the Seven Step, the music was divided 1-2-3-4 / 1-2-3. If you have music that sounds like that, and the tempo is slow enough, you can often dance Cross-Step Waltz like so:

Cross-Step Waltz in Slow 7/4 Time [SVS]

Counts	1	2	3	4	5	6	7 //	repeat
Steps	1		2	3 /	4	5	6 //	repeat

The first half is Cross-Step Foxtrot and the second half is Cross-Step Waltz.

In other cases, a song in 7/4 might be subdivided 1-2-3 / 1-2 / 1-2, as it is in "Méandres" from Cirque du Soleil. In these cases, you can dance a Cross-Step Foxtrot in which the slow step isn't quite as slow.

Cross-Step Waltz in Fast 7/4 Time [SVF]

```
Counts   123   12   12  /  123   12   12  //  repeat
Steps     1     2    3  /   4     5    6  //  repeat
```

∞

Fast 3/4 Time

When waltz music is faster than a comfortable walking tempo, Rotary Waltz is usually a better option. But when the tempo gets too fast for comfortable Rotary, Cross-Step Waltz can be danced once again by using a combination of the Hesitation Waltz (1—) and Canter Waltz (1–3) timings from the 1910s:

Hesitation Cross-Step Waltz [HCS]

```
Counts   1  2  3  /  4  5  6  /  1  2  3  /  4  5  6  //  repeat
Steps    1           2  3  /  4           5  6  //  repeat
```

This timing, and variations thereof, is also seen in Tango Vals and Bluesy Waltz (p. 207).

∞

Bottom Line: Cross-Step Waltz can be danced to a variety of different music using a variety of different strategies. The key, with any song, is to carefully listen to the music in order to find a logical and comfortable way to dance three/six steps to it. Let the music be your guide.

∞

Other timings are probably waiting to be discovered. If you find something that's particularly satisfying, let us know at: crossstepwaltz.com/share

"Creativity is allowing yourself to make mistakes.
Art is knowing which ones to keep."

— Scott Adams

Chapter 37

Letting It Happen

An excerpt from an essay by UT student Maya Josiam.

∞

I have been trained in South Indian classical dance, a style called Bharatanatyam, since I was six years old—I even compete with UT's Bharatanatyam team. When I started taking this class, so many of my friends would say to me, "Maya, this must be so easy for you since you're a dancer!" Boy, were they wrong.

Social dance has changed my perspective on what dance is and can be. I have spent so many years of my life knowing every second of a song and exactly what my whole body would be doing for the next two beats, two minutes, or even two hours. Every move was precisely choreographed: there was never room for error or for improvisation. Everyone was to be in total synchronization: even "interactions" on stage were rehearsed.

Social dance has shown me how hard it is to not only improvise, but to let someone else take the lead on what you're both doing together. I am learning how to relax and let the lead actually lead. Not only that, I have had to learn how to follow in the moment and not rely on a predetermined set of steps to guide me to the next motion.

As a person who considers herself a dancer, I have had to reexamine my definition of dance. "Life is a dance between making it happen and letting it happen," and dance is that as well. Staying on beat and knowing the basics: that's making it happen. But letting it happen is trusting your partner and yourself to create art and enjoyment simultaneously and spontaneously.

I'm usually pretty good at making it happen, but I am slowly getting comfortable with the idea of letting it happen. I would love to get to the point of being able to dance with a Lead and not constantly question if my foot is between his like water under a bridge or if I am turning in the right line of motion, but until then, I am learning to enjoy the process of learning.

"Life is a dance between
making it happen
and letting it happen."

— Arianna Huffington

Chapter 38

Transitions to Other Dances

Another benefit of Cross-Step Waltz is that it's easy to transition to and from a variety of other dances in waltz time. This allows you to diversify not only your Cross-Step Waltz, but your other dances as well.

Box Step Waltz

Box Step Waltz is usually danced to slower music than Cross-Step Waltz, but for in-between tempos, both dances are possible. Here's how you can transition between them:

Transition to Box Step Waltz [TBW]

(1-2-3) Dance half of a basic step, turning slightly CCW and squaring up the frame, then back the Follow into the first step of a Box Step on (4).

∞

Transition from Box Step Waltz [FBW]

(1-2-3) Dance half of a Box Step, drifting slightly away from each other, then lead into Cross-Step Waltz on (4).

This works best if you start it with the Lead facing the outside wall, so the primary cross-step is along LOD.

∞

The first transition allows you to diversify your Cross-Step Waltz by adding in figures based on the Box Step. The second transition not only allows you to get back to Cross-Step Waltz: it also allows you to dance Cross-Step Waltz figures with people who only know Box Step Waltz.

Several people we've done this with have told us that these figures feel similar to Silver Waltz (i.e., the Silver level of the American competition Waltz syllabus). So if you hear them talking about Silver, that's what they mean.

Adapted to 4/4 time, these transitions can also be used to transition between Cross-Step Foxtrot (p. 193) and Box Step Foxtrot.

∞

Rotary Waltz

Although Rotary Waltz is usually danced to faster music than Cross-Step Waltz, for in-between tempos, both dances are possible. Here are some easy transitions between them:

Walking Transition to Rotary Waltz [WTR]

(1-2-3) Three counts of Waltz Walk, then the Lead backs around into Rotary Waltz on (4), starting with Lead's left and Follow's right.

∞

Walking Transition from Rotary Waltz [WFR]

(1-2-3) Three counts of Waltz Walk, then cross into Cross-Step Waltz with Lead's right and Follow's left on (4).

Note that this requires you to underturn the last waltz to keep the Lead on the inside lane for the Waltz Walk on (1), rather than backing around as he usually would.

∞

If you'd rather turn more instead of less, here's a more advanced pair of transitions:

Pivot Transition to Rotary Waltz [PTR]

Cross (1), pivot (2), pivot (3), then back the Lead into the first step of Rotary Waltz on (4). The fourth step is essentially a third pivot step.

∞

Pivot Transition from Rotary Waltz [PFR]

Two 180° pivot steps, Lead backing (1), Follow backing (2), then step forward along LOD (3) and lead into the primary cross-step on (4). Think "pivot, pivot, aim."

All of the above transitions change the downbeat from (1) to (4). If you'd rather keep dancing on the (1), here are two transitions that allow you to do so:

Hesitating Transition to Rotary Waltz [HTR]

Cross (1), step side along LOD (2), hold (3), replace against LOD (4), hold (5-6), and start Rotary Waltz on (1).

This is similar to the Hesitating Side Sways (p. 20), but without stepping on (6).

Hesitating Transition from Rotary Waltz [HFR]

After a full turn of a Rotary Waltz, the Lead stays facing the outside wall for: a side step (1), swaying along LOD (2-3). Then a side step swaying against LOD (4-5), and replace weight onto the forward foot (6), leading into the primary cross-step of Cross-Step Waltz on (1).

Latin Waltz

Latin Waltz (also known as Swaltza), is Salsa in even timing (taking one step per beat) to waltz music. Almost any Salsa variation can be adapted into Latin Waltz.

Cross-Body Transition to Latin Waltz [TLW]

(1-2-3) Half of a basic step, turning slightly CCW and squaring up the frame, then back the Follow into the primary break step of Latin Waltz on (4).

If your CCW turn is 90°, you'll be dancing it straight along and against LOD.

Cross-Body Transition from Latin Waltz [FLW]

As the Follow does half of a Latin Waltz basic, the Lead breaks forward (1), replaces back (2), and steps side (3), forming a 90° angle with his partner (she's the base of a capital L and he's the ascender). This is the first half of a Cross-Body Lead in Latin Waltz.

Then simply lead into the primary cross-step of Cross-Step Waltz on (4).

Note that if you used the above entrance, you'll want to do something in Latin Waltz that turns you 180° (as many variations do), so that this transition has your primary cross-step traveling along LOD rather than against it.

Country Waltz

Country Waltz is the waltz-time version of Country Two Step, which begins by backing the Follow along LOD.

Transition to Country Waltz [TCW]

(1-2-3) Dance half of a basic step, turning 90° CCW and squaring up the frame, then back the Follow along LOD starting on (4).

Transition from Country Waltz [FCW]

(1-2-3) Back the Follow diagonally along LOD toward the outside wall while the Lead stays in the inside lane, "unsquaring" the frame into the crossbow position of Cross-Step Waltz, then lead into the primary cross-step on (4).

Swing Waltz

Swing Waltz (also known as Waltz Swing), is Nightclub Two Step in even timing to waltz music. Almost any Nightclub Two Step variation can be adapted into Swing Waltz.

Inside Turn Transition to Swing Waltz [TSW]

A Follow's inside turn along LOD on (2), catching in closed position for the primary side step of Swing Waltz (along LOD) on (4). The inside turn sets the Follow up to naturally fall back into the rock step on (5).

Outside Turn Transition from Swing Waltz [FSW]

(1-2-3) A Follow's outside turn along LOD into the primary cross-step on (4).

Note that the Follow will probably expect this to be a Spot Turn in Swing Waltz, so the Lead needs to clearly lead her (with leftward pressure from his right hand) to turn along LOD, pivoting forward, back, forward, rather than turning in place.

Adapted to 4/4 time, these transitions can also be used to transition between Cross-Step Foxtrot (p. 193) and Nightclub Two Step.

Hustle

While not the most traditional mashup, Cross-Step Waltz can also be mixed with three-count Hustle. This can be done to Hustle music (dancing threes across fours as in Hustle), or hard-hitting Cross-Step Waltz music (e.g. "Electric Feel" by MGMT).

Transition to Hustle [TTH]

From a CW Turning Basic in Cross-Step Waltz, simply lead into a CCW Turning Basic of Hustle on (1).

The key here is to clearly lead the "and-1" (in this case, the "and-4") after the first three counts to lead into the next three counts of Hustle, as the Follow will be expecting to continue stepping onto her R on (4), instead of restarting on her L.

∞

Transition from Hustle [TFH]

From a CCW Turning Basic in Hustle, simply lead into a CW Turning Basic in Cross-Step Waltz on (1) when you're lined up to cross along LOD.

Then clearly lead the smooth transition into the second half of the Turning Basic, as the Follow will be expecting to keep switching her feet every three counts as in Hustle.

∞

Mazurka Clandestina

Mazurka Clandestina is a recent evolution of the 19th century Mazurka. This new version is done late at night in the public squares of Europe, where dancers gather clandestinely to dance it to live folk music. The music is the same tempo as Cross-Step Waltz, which makes it easy to dance a fusion of the two.

Transition to Mazurka Clandestina [TMC]

Dance the Hesitating Transition to Rotary Waltz (p. 201), but instead of backing around, step side into the Mazurka step. This transition will keep you on the downbeat.

Transition from Mazurka Clandestina [FMC]

Dance the new Mazurka step: take a small side step with Lead's L and Follow's R (1), replace (2), bring free foot to supporting foot without weight, perhaps bouncing slightly (3).

Then lead into the second half of a Follow's Solo (p. 57) by the Lead's right side (4-5-6).

Continue into Cross-Step Waltz, clearly leading all six counts of a Turning Basic, since the Follow will likely expect the (1-2—4-5-6) timing of the Mazurka.

∞

A variety of Mazurka Clandestina figures are described starting on p. 211.

Chapter 39

Work and Play

Once upon a time, people had hobbies, like knitting, woodworking, and writing poetry. But in recent years, hobbies have been replaced by "side hustles." (This term first appeared in the 1950s, but has exploded in popularity in the past three years). If you believe the prevailing cultural opinion, you aren't a *real* craftsperson until you've sold your wares on Etsy, and you aren't a *real* poet unless you're published (self-publishing doesn't count).

Of course, there's nothing inherently wrong with making money from your passions: that's what all three of us are fortunate enough to do every day. But there's definitely something wrong if you feel you *need* to; that your hobby isn't "real" unless it's bringing in the dough. Contrary to popular belief, a hobby doesn't need to pay to be worthwhile: fun is reason enough to do something!

Unfortunately, in recent years, we've seen this popular hustling mentality begin to creep onto the dance floor. For example, in Austin, there's a thriving West Coast Swing scene. And while West Coast Swing is primarily a social dance, there's also a popular competition circuit, and many westies feel the need to compete. To prepare for competition, they attend every class and social across town, and then, with what little time they have left, they take expensive private lessons with the pros. While there's nothing fundamentally wrong with any of this as long as they're actually having fun, from our students' reports, many people are not. Some are even reaching the point of burnout and wanting to quit West Coast, or even dancing entirely!

Another one of our students told us that although they loved dancing, they had to stop because they didn't have enough time "to take it seriously enough to progress as a dancer." In this student's mind, it wasn't enough to simply have fun with their current skillset. If they weren't constantly improving as a dancer, it wasn't worth dancing at all.

Stories like these make us sad because, in our minds, dancing is supposed to be stress-relieving, not stress-inducing. But in recent years, we've seen a troubling shift—in a variety of different dance communities—toward treating dance as work instead of play.

Of course, this isn't to say that dancing is never work: it certainly can be when you're learning new things. But if working on new things in Cross-Step Waltz (or any dance) is stressing you out, that's the last thing we want to hear.

Fortunately, if you ever find yourself in this situation, we have an easy solution for you. It was given to us by Emily Huang, our amazing UT class assistant and a phenomenal West Coast Swing dancer who has shot up the ranks from Newcomer to All-Star in only two years. When we asked her how she did it, while remaining one of the sanest and sweetest people we know, here's what she had to say.

Rather than treating all of her dancing as work, she splits her time between work and play. Some songs, she consciously works on what she needs to work on based on recent competitions, private lessons, and personal goals, and other songs, she simply lets go and has fun. By consciously distinguishing between working dances and play dances, Emily has been able to maintain her passion for dancing while many of her peers have lost it.

Therefore, if you're the kind of dancer who's interested in working on your dancing, we recommend consciously making some dances working dances and other dances play dances, in which you let go of whatever you're working on at the moment and just dance. On the other hand, if you're the kind of dancer who just wants to dance, there's nothing wrong with making *every* dance a play dance! That is, after all, the ultimate goal of social dancing!

> "We don't stop playing because we grow old.
> We grow old because we stop playing."
>
> — George Bernard Shaw

Chapter 40

Bluesy Waltz / Waltz Fusion

Bluesy Waltz, also known as Waltz Fusion, is a way of dancing in 3/4 time that improvisationally combines elements from a wide variety of dance forms, including Blues, Tango, Swing, and of course, Waltz.

We're including it in this book because it's often danced at Cross-Step Waltz tempo, which makes it easy to incorporate elements of Cross-Step Waltz into it, and vice versa.

The Basic Idea

The basic idea of this dance form is to take whatever vocabulary you have as a dancer and find ways to improvisationally adapt it into waltz time, with a focus on musicality and connection.

Are you ready to dance it? If you're already enthusiastically saying "Yes," go for it! That may be all the direction you need. But if you'd like a bit more guidance first, we're happy to provide some in this chapter.

There are many different ways of approaching this dance. In fact, we might even go so far as to say that every couple who dances it will have their own unique style that is influenced by their combined vocabulary. For example, if you and your partner dance lots of Tango, your Bluesy Waltz may be more Tango-inspired, while another couple's Bluesy Waltz may be inspired by their background in West Coast Swing. (If you search for Bluesy Waltz and Waltz Fusion on YouTube, you'll find a variety of different dancers with variety of different interpretations, including Campbell Miller, Ari Levitt, and Nick and Melissa.)

As we noted before, musicality is key, so one good way to start thinking about this dance is to look at the different timings we can use when dancing in waltz time, and different steps that work well in these timings. But in doing so, it's important to note that by providing you with these sample timings and steps, we're not saying that this is all that's possible. Our goal is to inspire you to explore further by proposing ideas you may not have considered, rather than to limit you to dancing only what we've described.

1, 4

One way to interpret waltz music is simply to take slow steps on the downbeats: 1, 4, 1, 4.

Side Sways [BSW]

Elements of Waltz Fusion can be added to any existing waltz form, such as Cross-Step Waltz, in which case there isn't a basic step: you can simply go straight from Cross-Step Waltz into those Fusion elements. But if you want to dance Bluesy Waltz as the base form, here's the closest thing to a basic step it has: simply sway side to side.

(1) The Lead steps side L as the Follow steps side R, both swaying slightly into the step.

(4) The Lead steps side R as the Follow steps side L, both swaying slightly into the step.

This is a good way to synchronize with your partner and make sure you know what foot your partner is on. It's also a good base to come back to between bursts of creative improvisation.

In the middle of a dance, you can also start it with the second step (Lead's R, Follow's L), if that's the foot that's free.

It can also be done turning slightly CW.

∞

Given that Cross-Step Waltz starts on the Lead's R and Follow's L, and many of the steps described in this chapter begin on Lead's L and Follow's R, it will be useful to have an easy way to switch the feet. While there are many different ways you can do this in the course of the dance, here's a pair of easy transitions that you can use pretty much any time.

Transition from Cross-Step Waltz to Bluesy Waltz [CTB]

(1) Primary cross-step.

(2-3) Side step toward the hands (2), and hold (3), swaying toward the hands.

(4) Side step over the elbows into the second half of a Side Sway, and hold (5-6).

If you were dancing Cross-Step Waltz around the room, and want to play with Bluesy Waltz in place, make sure to get out of traffic into the center of the room before transitioning.

Transition from Bluesy Waltz to Cross-Step Waltz [BTC]

(1) Sway toward the hands.

(4) Sway toward the elbows.

(6) Step toward the hands in preparation for the primary cross-step.

If you were dancing Bluesy Waltz in the center of the room, and want to transition to an extended run of traveling Cross-Step Waltz, make sure your hands are pointed in a direction which will allow you to rejoin the CCW flow of traffic around the room.

But you don't necessarily need to transition fully back to traveling Cross-Step Waltz. You can also use this transition to add elements of Cross-Step Waltz to your Bluesy Waltz while remaining in the center of the room.

∞

1-2-3, 4 or 1, 4-5-6

Bluesy Waltz can be danced to any music in waltz time, but it's particularly nice when you dance it to bluesy waltz music, like "Not the Same" by Mingo Fishtrap. (For a longer list of recommended music, see p. 219.)

Bluesy waltz music often has an emphasized downbeat:

$$\mathbf{1}\ 2\ 3\ /\ \mathbf{4}\ 5\ 6$$

Therefore, it often makes sense to emphasize this downbeat with your dancing, perhaps by hesitating on it: 1-2-3, 4; or 1, 4-5-6. You dance four steps—any four steps—holding on either the fourth step or the first one. For the historically-inclined, this timing is essentially a modern version of the 1910s Hesitation Waltz.

Here are some particularly satisfying variations in this timing.

Waltz and Hesitate [BWH]

(1-2-3) The first half of a Rotary Waltz, with the Lead backing around L.

(4) A hesitating side step over the elbows, holding (5-6).

This can also be done with Reverse Waltz, turning to the left, in which case the Follow backs around R on (1-2-3). The hesitation is still to the elbows side.

It can also be done hesitating forward/back instead of to the side. In the Rotary version, the Lead will hesitate forward R as the Follow hesitates back L. In the Reverse version, the Lead will hesitate back R as the Follow hesitates forward L.

Note: For a detailed description of Rotary and Reverse Waltz, see *Waltzing*.

Hesitate and Waltz [BHW]

(1) A hesitating side step over the hands, holding (2-3).

(4-5-6) The second half of a Rotary Waltz, with the Follow backing around L.

This can also be done with Reverse Waltz, turning to the left, in which case the Lead backs around R on (4-5-6).

It can also be done hesitating forward/back instead of to the side. In the Rotary version, the Lead hesitates back L as the Follow hesitates forward R. In the Reverse version, the Lead hesitates forward L as the Follow hesitates back R.

Hesitating Pivots [BHP]

In any of the variations above, you can replace the Rotary Waltz with three pivot steps, turning more dramatically on the spot.

Backing Hesitation [BBH]

(1-2-3-4) Back the Follow four steps, hesitating on the fourth.

Or back the Lead four steps, hesitating on the fourth.

A nice combination is to back one partner, then back the other.

Grapevine Hesitation [BGH]

(1-2-3-4) Four steps of a grapevine, hesitating on the fourth. For example, side (1), Lead crosses behind as Follow crosses in front (2), side (3), Lead crosses in front as the Follow crosses behind (4), and hold (5-6).

(1-2-3-4) Return to place with: Lead replaces back onto L, a cross behind, as the Follow replaces forward onto R, a cross in front (1), side (2), Lead crosses in front as the Follow crosses behind (3), and step side to where you originally started (4), and hold (5-6).

Other Grapevine Hesitations are possible, but that's a particularly nice combination.

∞

Leg Flare [BLF]

(1-2-3) Three CW pivot steps on the spot, Lead backing, Follow backing, Lead backing.

(4) The Follow takes one more pivot step on her L while the Lead dramatically stops and allows the frame to open, as he slightly lifts up the frame to allow her R leg to flare out CW. She'll eventually fall back onto her R, which leaves her L free to cross into something.

∞

1-2, 4-5-6 or 1-2-3, 4-5

This is the timing of the weight changes in the 19th century Mazurka. While the original Mazurka is still danced in vintage dance communities today, it has also recently evolved into a more relaxed version, Mazurka Clandestina. This new version is done late at night in the public squares of Europe, where dancers gather clandestinely to dance it to live folk music.

Everything from Mazurka Clandestina can be incorporated into Bluesy Waltz. Here are a few of our favorite variations in this timing.

∞

Mazurka and Waltz [BMW]

(1-2-3) Dance the new Mazurka step: take a small side step with Lead's L and Follow's R (1), replace (2), bring free foot to supporting foot without weight, perhaps bouncing slightly (3).

(4-5-6) First half of a "Rotary Waltz," turning either CW or CCW. The Rotary Waltz is in quotes because it doesn't have to be a half-turning traveling waltz, although it also can be.

(1-2-3) Repeat the Mazurka step on the other foot, over the elbows.

(4-5-6) Second half of a "Rotary Waltz," turning either CW or CCW.

Two Mazurkas, Two Waltzes [BMM]

(1-6) Two Mazurka steps over the hands.

(1-6) A full "Rotary Waltz," turning either CW or CCW.

∞

Two Mazurkas, Waltz, and Tango Close [BMC]

The second bar of Waltz can be replaced with a Tango Close in Mazurka timing: step side over the elbows (4) and close free foot without weight (5), holding (6).

∞

Three Mazurkas and Waltz [BKO]

(1-9) Three Mazurka steps over the hands.

(10-12) First half of a "Rotary Waltz," turning either CW or CCW.

Repeat the whole thing on the other foot, for a total of eight bars.

This is the timing of the 19th century La Koska.

∞

Mazurka and Pivot [BMP]

In any of the above variations, the "Rotary Waltz" counts can be replaced by three more dramatically turning pivot steps in place.

∞

Pivoting Basic [BPB]

In some communities, this is considered the basic step of Mazurka Clandestina.

(1-2-3) Mazurka step over the hands.

(4-5-6) Wind the Follow up CCW: she steps side (4), rocks behind (5), and replaces forward (6) as the Lead steps side, breaks forward, and replaces back.

(1-2-3) A CW pivot in place, Follow backing around L (1), Lead backing around L (2), and hold (3), perhaps with a slight lift to prevent the Follow from taking weight.

(4-5-6) The second half of a "Rotary Waltz," turning CW in place.

Pivoting Basic with Tango Close [BPT]

The final three counts of the Pivoting Basic can be replaced with a Tango Close in Mazurka timing: step side over the elbows (4) and close free foot without weight (5), holding (6).

∞

Grapevine Catch with Tango Close [BGC]

(1-2-3) Mazurka step over the hands.

(4-5-6) Three-count grapevine over the hands: side (4), Lead crosses behind as the Follow crosses in front (5), side (6).

(1-2-3) Catch in the fourth step of a grapevine, with the Follow crossing behind while the Lead crosses in front (1), and hold, perhaps dipping slightly (2), then replace back/forward out of the cross (3).

(4-5) Finish with a Tango Close in Mazurka timing.

∞

Grapevine Gancho [BGG]

(1-6) Same as above.

(1-2-3) The Lead crosses in front as the Follow crosses behind, but the Lead plants his R behind the Follow's free R foot, right hip to right hip (1). Continuing her momentum, but unable to step back right, the Follow does a Gancho, quickly sliding her right calf up the Lead's right calf to lock knees with him (2). Then she unhooks her right knee from his, and, optionally, hooks it in front of her own left knee (3).

(4-5-6) The Follow steps forward R back toward where they came from (4) and side L, perhaps turning CW on those two steps, as the Lead rocks back L out of his earlier R cross (4), and steps forward R between her feet (5). Hold (6).

∞

Two Mazurkas, Grapevine and Close [BMG]

(1-6) Two Mazurka steps over the hands.

(1-2-3) A mirrored grapevine over the elbows: both cross behind (1), step side (2), and cross in front (3).

(4-5) Finish with a Tango Close in Mazurka timing.

Follow's Solo Rueda [BFR]

(1-2-3) Mazurka step over the hands.

(4-5-6) The Lead sends the Follow CW by his right pocket into second half of the Follow's Solo as in Cross-Step Waltz, as he does a Back Ocho, crossing behind.

(1-2-3) He starts to lead the Follow into a Grapevine Rueda CCW around him, as he turns CCW in place, tracking her. She crosses in front (1), then steps side (2), and holds (3). Leads, be clear to lead this hold, perhaps with a slight lift.

(4-5-6) Finish the Grapevine Rueda. She crosses behind (4), steps side (5), and crosses in front (6), continuing to travel CCW around him, as he continues to turn in place. The more you rotate this CCW, the better.

During a class in Mazurka, one of our class assistants, Sofia Valdivieso-Sinyakov, noticed that if you keep the Grapevine Rueda going for two more cycles of Mazurka (1-2, 4-5-6, 1-2, 4-5-6), it also resolves, for a **Longer Follow's Solo Rueda** [BFL]. Each hold is at a different point in the Grapevine: first, it's before she crosses behind, then before she steps side, then before she crosses in front.

∞

Media Luna Vai Ven [BVV]

This is inspired by a Tango figure in Nicanor Lima's *El Tango Argentino de Salon* from Buenos Aires, c. 1916.

(1-2-3) Mazurka step over the hands.

(4-5-6) Back the Follow three steps, stopping on the third.

(1-2-3) The Lead sweeps his R around from back to front, like a windshield wiper, as the Follow sweeps her L from front to back. On (3), start to sweep the feet back to where they came from.

(4-5-6) Finish with the second half of a "Rotary Waltz," turning CW in place.

Alternatively, the Follow can step around the Lead onto her L on (4), then sweep her R out and around CW on (5-6), as the Lead provides support by circling her CW, for a **Media Luna Vai Ven with Carousel Ending** [BVC].

∞

These are just a few of our favorite variations in this timing: there are many other things you can do, so feel free to get creative!

1, 3

This is another useful timing you can use, borrowed from the 1910s Canter Waltz.

Take one slow step (1), holding (2), then one quick step (3). This keeps you on the same foot, so it's good for steps that repeat in sets of two, e.g., pivots, grapevines, walking. For example:

Canter Pivots [BCP]

Do pivots, either in place, or traveling, Lead backing on (1) and Follow backing on (3).

∞

The fact that a canter step keeps you on the same foot is also good if you want to change the downbeat. For example, if the Lead's L and Follow's R are free on (1), after a standard (1) or (1-2-3), you'll have the Lead's R and Follow's L free on (4). But if you want to keep the same foot free to do something on that foot on (4), you can use a canter step to keep that foot free. The transition from Bluesy Waltz to Cross-Step Waltz at the beginning of this chapter takes advantage of this principle.

∞

Canter timing can also be combined with Waltz timing, i.e., 1, 3, 4-5-6, or 1-2-3, 4, 6—which gives you five steps to play with over six counts.

Or it can be combined with a hesitation—1, 3, 4 or 1, 4, 6—which gives you three steps to play with over six counts.

Another fun timing to play with is an AABA sequence in which A is a waltz or hesitation, and B is a canter: 1-2-3, 4-5-6, 1-3, 4-5-6, or 1, 4, 1-3, 4. This can also be repeated opposite, doing something in AABA timing on one foot, then doing the same thing on the other foot.

∞

While we could describe a variety of other fun variations that utilize canter timing, we'll leave you the satisfaction of discovering them yourself!

Dips and Tricks

Another significant part of Bluesy Waltz are moves that people often categorize as "Dips and Tricks." While we've already described many satisfying moves of this variety both in this chapter (Leg Flare, Grapevine Gancho, and Media Luna Vai Ven) and the Endings chapter (p. 151), here are a few more dip and trick options that are particularly satisfying in Bluesy Waltz.

Carousel [CAR]

This Tango-inspired move is one of Campbell Miller's favorites in Bluesy Waltz.

The Lead steps out to his left side while clearly leading the Follow to step onto her R and stay there throughout the entire figure. Then he circles her CW while supporting her rotation on her R. Her free L foot can sweep along the floor to her side, or slightly in front or behind her.

Exit with a side step toward the elbows side onto the Follow's free foot.

∞

Monkey Bars [MON]

Nick and Melissa first learned this West Coast Swing move for the 2013 Viennese Ball Opening Committee Waltz choreographed by Joachim De Lombaert and Kseniya Charova, where they danced it in a wedding dress and tails.

From closed position, the Lead places his left hand on top of the Follow's right shoulder and sends her through the tunnel of the frame under his right arm. The Follow takes her right hand and hooks onto his right arm or shoulder from below, and swings under his right arm, using it like a monkey bar. While she's actually stepping through, and not fully swinging from his arm, the Lead should be ready to support her with a solid right arm.

After she passes under, it's easy to slide away to right-to-left hands to lead something from there. A particularly nice combination is to lead straight into a Free Spin Dip (p. 154), for a **Monkey Bars to Free Spin Dip** [MOD].

In addition to dipping after Monkey Bars, you can also lead into Monkey Bars from a Dip. To lead a **Dip in Bluesy Waltz** [BDP], simply take a side step into the dip. It's like a Tango Dip in Cross-Step Waltz (p. 152), but without the cross-step first.

From the Dip, you can send the Follow under the Lead's right arm into Monkey Bars, for a **Dip to Monkey Bars** [DMB]. When the music supports it, Melissa will often initiate this from the Follow's role. If Nick dips her, and there's another musical flourish right after it, she'll take her right arm from his left shoulder and hook it under his right arm to send herself straight into Monkey Bars.

1-2-3, 4-5-6

In addition to playing with all of the different kinds of hesitations described above, you can also simply take one step per beat: 1-2-3, 4-5-6.

Using this timing, you can dance any variation from any dance in waltz time, including:

- Cross-Step Waltz
- Rotary Waltz
- Latin Waltz
- Swing Waltz
- Box Step Waltz
- Country Waltz

Another fun option is to adapt the Fox-Blues variations that evolved into Cross-Step Waltz into waltz time. For descriptions of those variations, see "The French Valse Boston" on p. 79.

At first, you might think of each of these waltzes as different lands you can visit in the course of a song. For example, you might do a bit of Cross-Step Waltz, then a bit of Latin Waltz, then a bit of Swing Waltz, then a bit of Fox-Blues.

But as you get more comfortable with the idea of Bluesy Waltz, it's also fun to break things down further, and mix and match dance forms on a variation-by-variation basis, rather than taking an extended vacation in any one land. You transition straight from one move in one dance to another move in another dance, treating every variation of every waltz as a variation of a new dance called Bluesy Waltz, rather than a variation of a different dance form that must be transitioned into before you can dance it.

The next step down this path is borrowing little bits of vocabulary from various dances, without necessarily dancing any complete variation as it exists in its original dance form. The bits you borrow can be partial variations, or even just concepts, like a cross-body lead or a free spin. Rather than thinking in whole variations, just see what flows naturally from where you are, moment-by-moment, step-by-step. This has a completely different feeling than just leading and following whole variations as you already know them.

Putting It All Together

In this chapter, we've explored a variety of different timings you can use in Bluesy Waltz.

To review, there are four common one-bar timings:

- 1
- 1-2-3
- 1-2
- 1, 3

Each of these can be mixed and matched to form a variety of two-bar timings, including:

- 1, 4
- 1, 4-5-6
- 1-2-3, 4
- 1-2, 4-5-6
- 1-2-3, 4-5
- 1-2, 4-5
- 1, 3, 4, 6
- 1, 3, 4-5-6
- 1-2-3, 4, 6
- 1, 3, 4
- 1, 4, 6
- 1-2-3, 4-5-6

Just as all of the dances in waltz time can be thought of as lands you can visit, so can the timings. At first, you can stay in each land for a while, seeing what you can create in one timing, before moving onto another one. Then you can experiment with mixing timings on a variation-by-variation basis. And finally, you can mix the timings moment-by-moment, step-by-step.

If the thought of that is too overwhelming, there are two essential things to help guide you, the dual *raisons d'être* of the dance: connection and musicality.

Connection in Bluesy Waltz

The first goal of this dance is connection.

Therefore, Leads, rather than trying to plan out what you're going to do in advance, just let things evolve step-by-step, allowing the Follow's momentum to guide you. Don't overthink it: just lead the most comfortable next step for her, whatever that will be.

Similarly, Follows, just let things evolve step-by-step, taking the most comfortable next step, rather than trying to guess the whole variation. If the Lead is following the above advice, even he doesn't know what the end of the variation will look like yet: he'll decide what comes next based on what you do now!

Musicality in Bluesy Waltz

The second goal of this dance is musicality.

In the ideal Bluesy Waltz, the dance will be an equal three-way partnership between the Lead, the Follow, and the music. Rather than giving you more theory about this (if you want the theory, see Chapter 15), it'll be more useful to put it into practice.

Wherever you prefer to listen to music, pull up "Gravity" by John Mayer, a classic bluesy waltz.

As you listen to the song, take a look at the list of timings on the previous page, and count them over the music. You can go straight down the list, or bounce around at random: the idea is simply to get used to hearing each of these timings in the music.

If you listen to the song repeatedly and get to know it, you may begin to hear certain parts of the song certain ways, i.e, "this part of the song sounds like this timing." Ideally, as you dance, you'll match your dancing to the music.

But this is just the ultimate ideal. Fortunately, as you learned while counting out the music, most of those timings actually fit most parts of the song, or at least count as satisfying alternate interpretations of what the music is saying. So as long as you're doing something that respects the music, and allows you to meaningfully connect with your partner, you're dancing Bluesy Waltz successfully!

∞

Bluesy Waltz Music

For a Spotify playlist of these songs, visit: crossstepwaltz.com/bluesy

- "Not the Same" by Mingo Fishtrap
- "The Air That I Breathe" by Maroon 5
- "If I Ain't Got You" by Alicia Keys
- "Gravity" by John Mayer
- "Earned It" by The Weeknd
- "Stop" by Sheryl Crow
- "A Beautiful Mess" by Jason Mraz
- "Dazed & Confused" by Ruel
- "Can't Let You Go" by Matchbox Twenty
- "Is This Love" by Corinne Bailey Rae

"When you dance, your purpose is not to get to a certain place on the floor. It's to enjoy each step along the way."

— Wayne Dwyer

Chapter 41

Discography of Cross-Step Waltz Music

There are many songs for dancing Cross-Step Waltz.

The following list includes some of our favorites that can be danced through without editing. For a Spotify playlist of these songs, visit: crossstepwaltz.com/music

- "All the Pretty Little Horses" by Kukuruza
- "Falling off the Face of the Earth" by Matt Wertz
- "Leaves of October" by Andrea Perry
- "Can't Take My Eyes Off You" by Lady Antebellum
- "Isabella's Lullaby" from The Promised Neverland Soundtrack
- "I Miss You" by Incubus
- "Devil In My Veins" by Yelawolf
- "Hurricane" by The Likes of Us
- "Felitsa" by Yanni
- "I Will Send For You" by Christel Alsos
- "Vanderlyle Crybaby Geeks" by The National
- "Drømmevei" by Anders Jektvik
- "The Blue River Waltz" by Jay Ungar & Molly Mason
- "NO EXCUSES" by NEEDTOBREATHE
- "Lucky" by Bif Naked
- "Hoy, Small Fry! (Remix)" by Hyperduck Soundworks
- "An American Quilt" by Thomas Newman
- "Love" by Corey Crowder
- "Lore of the Loom" by Secret Garden
- "Blue Eyes" by Cary Brothers

Found a new Cross-Step Waltz song we should hear? Let us know at: crossstepwaltz.com/share

About the Authors

Richard Powers is a social dance instructor and historian at Stanford University. Richard's focus since 1975 has been the research and reconstruction of American and European social dance forms, working from a personal collection of over two thousand historic dance manuals.

Richard's grandfather taught social dance at Virginia Polytechnic Institute and his parents met at a swing dance. At Stanford, he was a student in the early years of the Product Design program. He also was one of the first students to pursue an individually designed major. He graduated from Stanford with a Master's degree in design and the creative process.

He moved to Cincinnati, Ohio, where he was Vice President of Genesis Design Group and did freelance design work for other companies. He holds eight U.S. and international patents, and was the recipient of 25 Art Directors awards for graphic and multimedia design. While in Cincinnati, he founded the artist's collective Co-Works, and received the Post-Corbett Award for Artist of the Year, Cincinnati's foremost arts recognition. He exhibited his multimedia constructions at The Contemporary Arts Center and at the Cincinnati Arts Consortium. He also founded the Clifton Court Dancers (Renaissance and Baroque dance), the Flying Cloud Academy of Vintage Dance (19th and 20th century dance), and the Fleeting Moments Waltz & Quickstep Orchestra.

Richard became a full-time instructor at Stanford University's Dance Division, joining the faculty in 1992. He was selected by the Centennial Issue of Stanford Magazine as one of Stanford University's most notable graduates of its first century, and was awarded the Lloyd W. Dinkelspiel Award for distinctive and exceptional contributions to education at Stanford University.

Richard has choreographed for dozens of stage productions, including Broadway and off-Broadway, and for films and television. He has taught over five hundred dance workshops across the U.S. and abroad.

On October 23, 2016, Richard was honored to be the Officiant presiding over the wedding of Nick and Melissa Enge.

You can find further information, including Richard's workshop schedule, photos, and examples of his design and illustration, at: http://richardpowers.com

∞

Nick & Melissa Enge are social dance instructors, historians, and anthropologists at the University of Texas at Austin, where they teach and research a wide variety of partnered social dance forms from the 19th century to present and around the world.

Nick and Melissa met each other in the Stanford social dance community after taking Richard's classes. At the time, Nick was studying Atmosphere/Energy Engineering and Melissa was studying Linguistics, but both found an even greater passion in social dance and the many ways it can change people's lives. After assisting Richard's classes at Stanford for five years, they were fortunate to be given the opportunity to teach their own at UT.

When not in class, Nick can be found maintaining the Library of Dance (libraryofdance.org), an ever-growing collection of dance manuals, reconstructions, and demo videos. His bibliography of dance manuals (libraryofdance.org/manuals) includes over 5,000 sources, 1,600 of which are available as free downloads. In addition, Nick has indexed 3,000 of these sources, creating a searchable database of the dances and variations contained in each source. Working from these sources, as well as their field research, Nick and Melissa have reconstructed thousands of variations and filmed over 2,500 demo videos of dances both vintage and modern.

Of particular note is their Early Tango project, in which they reconstructed nearly every Tango variation known to have been published in the first decade of its global popularity (the 1910s), and created demo videos of all of them in period attire in a period ballroom at the Davenport Hotel in Spokane. You can find it at: libraryofdance.org/dances/early-tango

When not in class, Melissa can be found helping people get jobs as a Quality Assurance Engineer at Indeed. In addition to teaching people to communicate non-verbally at UT, Nick and Melissa also work together to teach people to communicate verbally by giving frequent public speaking workshops at Indeed. Last year, Nick and Melissa published a research-based guide to public speaking best practices entitled *The Science of Speaking*.

Acknowledgments

From Richard:

This book is built upon a foundation of many talented and inspiring people. What appears to be the work of three authors is actually a life-long collaboration of friends and colleagues from many disciplines.

Nick and Melissa Enge are always a joy to work with. They have an increasing range of experience in teaching, dancing, and writing, and this book wouldn't have been possible without them. I have enjoyed the energy of our daily exchanges of ideas and feedback, the chapters that they contributed are essential, and their videos of the variations are an invaluable part of the book.

The impetus for writing this book was a request by the participants at the third annual Crystal Dragon Cross-Step Waltz Festival in Saint Petersburg, Russia. On the first day of the week-long festival, July 1, 2019, they asked for an entire book on Cross-Step Waltz. I asked Nick and Melissa if they'd be interested in co-writing it, and they immediately said yes. By the end of that month, we had completed a 180-page first draft.

Maren Shemshourenko directs the Crystal Dragon Dance Studio in Saint Petersburg, and has created an amazing dance community. They not only love Cross-Step Waltz, but they also the spirit of creativity, flexibility, individuality, connection, and kindness that are embodied in Cross-Step Waltz. The positive influence of Maren and the Crystal Dragon community is manifested throughout this book, in many ways. Maren and Aleksey Chernyak are also a part of a publishing company, and intend to translate this book into Russian and publish it. I also appreciate the pioneering work that Alexey Nelyubov, Georgiy Shulpin, Ksenia Balakireva, Pavel Kozlov, and Yulia Bojarskaya are doing to expand the success of Cross-Step Waltz in Russia.

I am grateful for the continual support and assistance of my wife Tracey. Many people agree that she is the best teammate ever, in so many ways, including help with information technology (she is a software engineer at Google), and helping me work out many of these waltz variations. I am very blessed to have Tracey as my life teammate.

Every time that someone comments on my positive outlook on life, I immediately give credit to my mom, Janet ("Tommy") Powers, who continues (at the age of 97) to be an inspiration and prototype for actively appreciating what is good in life, in art, and in people. I'm grateful to both of my parents, for being the best possible exemplars for leading a fulfilling life.

Angela Amarillas has been more than my teaching partner for the past twenty-five years. She has been a continual part of the process of developing both the ideas and dances described in this book. I'm also appreciative of the very helpful feedback from Mirage Marrou Greene and Melissa Enge, my teaching partners for the past decade. Mirage partnered the Waltz Lab as well, and co-created many of its variations. Both Melissa and Nick Enge were in all of my classes for many years, and helped shape Cross-Step Waltz and its variations at Stanford. Currently, Rocky Aikens is doing a stellar job of partnering my Stanford classes, with her valuable feedback for both the teaching and the shaping of Cross-Step Waltz. Then when I teach in Russia, I am grateful for the superb partnering of Ekaterina "Enchie" Bulchuk and Olga Savelyeva.

Joan Walton has been a long-time collaborator in the art of teaching dance. I've enjoyed working with Joan for the past thirty-five years, exchanging ideas on ways to present such ephemeral material as clearly as possible.

I would like to thank Sid Hetzler for providing the inspiration and "home away from home" for the first decade of waltz weekends, which featured Cross-Step Waltz. Sid also let me use his writer's cabin in Georgia, where I wrote the first draft of some concepts in this book.

I thank my many friends and students who have passed on their favorite waltz music over the decades, especially Timmie Wong, who composed and recorded many waltzes, and Lucas Garron, who developed a Python script for turning almost any recording into a waltz.

We thank Manuel Avendano and Tam King for contributing their beautiful artwork to this book. We would also like to thank our students for letting us quote their class essays in this book. And thanks to Kristina Vannoni and Joan Walton for their proofreading.

A vast coalition of dancers contributed to the creation and development of the variations described in this book. The list could go on forever but must include James Mendoza, Ryan and Monica Shen Knotts, Campbell Miller, Georgiy ("Rold") Shulpin, Lilli Ann and Claire Carey, Zachariah Cassady, Susan de Guardiola, Bill Boling and Beata Csanadi, Peggy Leiby and Ret Turner, Alexey Nelyubov, Tim Lamm and Paula Harrison, Timmie Wong, Sven Jensen, Lucas Garron, Donald Harvey, George Yang, and Ari Levitt, plus over a hundred more innovators in the Waltz Lab. I am also indebted to a few dancers in particular who set a prototype for exceptionally creative approaches to dance and "coloring outside the lines." These include Steve Kreimer, Frank Clayton, Deb Henigson, Walter Dill, and Andy Jewell.

These acknowledgements would not be complete without mentioning Josette Courtade, Sylvie and Jean-Pierre Orgeret, Jean-François Lafitte and Andrée Gamelin, who showed me the traditional French version of Cross-Step Waltz (which happens to be identical to our version). Knowledge of historical traditions give an added depth to any dance form.

Finally, I wish to thank all of my students that I've had the honor of teaching for the past few decades. Each class has been a two-way exchange, and I have learned much from each session. Thank you for your feedback and inspiration.

From Melissa:

Starting at the beginning, I have to give a big thank you to Art of Motion and Inspirations dance studios in Bartlesville, Oklahoma. Without Shelly Beech, Shannon Fox, and their respective talented teams, I never would have discovered the pure joy that is dance.

After an injury, I was told I couldn't keep dancing, and I forgot that joy until I came to Stanford and became one of the lucky few freshmen to get into Social Dance I. Almost instantly, everything positive and amazing about dancing came rushing back to me! Thanks, Richard, for helping me rediscover something that truly makes my soul sing.

In elementary school, I was asked to write about "goals for my life." My goal was to become a dance teacher. Fast-forward to my senior year, when I got an email from Richard asking if I was interested in being his teaching partner. So thank you, Richard, for making my childhood dream come true! I've learned so much from you, about history, about dance, and about life itself. And I'm still learning from you to this day.

My next thanks go to Mirage Marrou Greene. She was Richard's teaching assistant when I took the classes, and I idolized her. A few years later, I was so excited for the opportunity to partner her classes. We ended up becoming incredibly close friends, and she was the most perfect maid of honor I could've ever asked for. I'm incredibly thankful for the great conversations, laughs, and moments we've shared over the years and the many more surely to come!

I'm eternally grateful to my mom, Brenee Carvell, for her love and support my whole life. Almost every recital I had as a child featured her as one of the backstage moms, and no one else could have transformed 40-some-odd jazz ponytails into sleek ballet buns like she did! Now that I'm older, she's become one of my best friends, always happy to chat, lend an ear, or dance around the living room :) Love you, Mom!

I'm equally grateful to my dad, Lee Carvell, who always encouraged me to pursue what made me happy, whether it was engineering, writing, running, or dance. Fun fact: he led me through my first Polka at a cousin's wedding! And more recently, our father-daughter salsa dance is a memory I'll cherish forever both because of the wonderful fun we had but also because he surprised me with moves I didn't know he knew :) Love you, Dad!

My final thanks go to Nick. You've been so many things to me over the years—an awesome dance partner, a ray of sunshine on a dark day, a brilliant colleague, and of course a loving, supportive boyfriend-fiancé-husband. Just by being your confident, happy self, you've challenged me to grow and become a better person: for that, I'm eternally grateful. I love doing life with you and am always looking forward to our next adventure. Love you, dear!

From Nick:

In so many ways, Melissa and I wouldn't be where we are today without Richard. In addition to teaching us social dance, Richard indirectly introduced us to each other through the Stanford dance community. Being a part of Richard's teaching team brought us closer together, and several years later, he officiated our wedding. Although we now live half a country away, Melissa and I are still honored and delighted to be working with him on an ever-changing array of dance projects. We can't thank you enough, Richard, for all you've given us, and all that you've done for the field of social dancing!

We also want to give thanks to Campbell Miller for establishing the current social dance program at UT, and for recommending us to carry on her amazing legacy. Without her pioneering work here, the UT social dance program wouldn't be the same. We are also grateful to Michael Sanders and John Bartholomew for giving us the opportunity to teach here.

In our classes at UT, we are blessed to have the assistance of an army of class assistants (CAs), who not only help our students become better dancers, but also help us become better teachers. A big thank you to our past and current CAs, Tommy Anthony, Brent Atchison, Chi Bao, Tara Caminade, Ben Chaiprasert, Kevin Chin, Paul Choi, Schuyler Christensen, Dara Cline, Jordan Cline, Talía Colón, Koger Darden, Cooper Fryar, Joseph Gonzales, Caroline Hao, Emily Huang, Roland Ip, Rissa Jackson, Emma Jaud, Rachel Kao, Joseph Kim, Seongyong Kim, Cinnamon Kiser, Tai Lewis, Vanessa Li, Sergio Limas, Samantha Lin, Jerry Liu, Alan Lo, Arushii Nadar, Melanie Nguyen, Catherine Parish, Ashley Pham, Ben Phung, Katie Phung, Sindhu Reddy, Molly-Marie Richards, Katelyn Ripkowski, Alex Robles, Roshini Saravanakumar, Tyler Schattel, Rohan Small, Elizabeth Smith, Lisa Strong, Stephanie Su, Kevin Sung, Geoffrey Tian, Abby Gail Triño, Sofia Valdivieso-Sinyakov, Rohit Venugopal, Andrew Vernon, Becky Weishuhn, Tommy Wilczek, and Jasmine Wong, and all the CAs we will have in the future.

Specifically, we want to thank Cooper Fryar for helping us set up our demo videos for this book, Tommy Anthony, Cooper Fryar, Rissa Jackson, and Sofia Valdivieso-Sinyakov for providing variations, and our current CAs for demoing some of the Creative Interpretations.

We also want to thank all of the dancers we've had the honor of teaching over the years. We can honestly say that we've learned just as much from you as you've learned from us.

Writing a book can be a lonely endeavor, but our cat Mistinguette (Misty for short, named after the inventor of the Apache dance) was always there to keep us company, and even made a cameo appearance in our Fox-Blue videos. If you happen to find a random string of characters in the book, it's probably because she stepped on the keyboard when we weren't looking ;)

Per and Elaine Enge are the best parents I could possibly imagine. They have given me all I could hope for in life and more, and have supported me every step of the way, enabling me to achieve my wildest dreams. And as they could tell you, I've had some pretty wild dreams.

Finally, I want to thank Melissa, for being an amazing partner in every way and in every arena. Everything in life is better with you and I'm so glad that we're able to do so much together, from dancing and teaching to cooking and traveling. Here's to a lifetime of continuing to be #couplegoals ;) I love you!

Image Credits

p. 2 — courtesy of Yulia Bojarskaya

pp. 8, 92 — illustrations by Nick Enge

p. 13 — illustration by Tamarind King

p. 18 — photo from *Modern Dancing* (1914) by Vernon & Irene Castle

pp. 79, 80, 82, 83 — from the collection of Richard Powers

p. 91 — illustration by Wikipedia user Martin Grandjean (SlvrKy)

p. 94 — screenshot from Google Search

p. 180 — photo by Wikipedia user EncMstr

p. 181 — photo by flickr user James Jones (puggles)

This book is set primarily in ITC Garamond,
drawn in 1977 by Tony Stan for the International Typeface Corporation (ITC).
The cover and title page are set in Wisteria ITC and Cochin.
It is published by Redowa Press in Stanford, California,
and printed on-demand by Kindle Direct Publishing.

This book is set primarily in ITC Garamond,
drawn in 1977 by Tony Stan for the International Typeface Corporation (ITC).
The cover and title page are set in Wisteria ITC and Cochin.
It is published by Redowa Press in Stanford, California,
and printed on-demand by Kindle Direct Publishing.

www.ingramcontent.com/pod-product-compliance
Lightning Source LLC
Chambersburg PA
CBHW080538170426
43195CB00016B/2598